WILD
INDIA

WILD INDIA

The wildlife and scenery of India and Nepal

━◀ ● ● ● ▶━

Photographs by **GERALD CUBITT**
Text by **GUY MOUNTFORT**

NEW
HOLLAND

Acknowledgements

Many people assisted us in the preparation of this book, contributing both moral and practical support. The interest shown by the Chief Wildlife Wardens and Chief Conservators of Forests in the State Governments, and the enthusiasm of the Directors of the many protected areas we visited provided invaluable encouragement during our travels. We acknowledge this help with gratitude and regret only that the individuals who assisted us are too numerous to mention here.

We would, however, like to make particular mention of the following organizations and government bodies for their valuable contribution to the success of the project: the Indian Board for Wildlife; the International Union for Conservation of Nature and Natural Resources; the World Wide Fund for Nature (India); and the World Wide Fund for Nature (International); the Data Centre for Natural Resources, Bangalore; the Welcomgroup Hotels; Indian Airlines; Tiger Tops Mountain Travel (Pvt) Ltd; the India Tourism Development Corporation; the Royal Botanic Gardens, Kew; the Natural History Museum, London.

Special thanks are due to Shri Samar Singh, Joint Secretary, Wildlife, in the Department of the Environment, and his deputy, for their advice and practical assistance. Shri Samar Singh earned our extra gratitude for his kind co-operation in reading the manuscript and ensuring the accuracy of the text. Special thanks are also due to Shri Hemendra Panwar, Director: Project Tiger, and Peter Jackson, who gave us the benefit of his long experience as a naturalist and wildlife photographer in India. Our grateful thanks also go to Dr Michael J. B. Green, Head, Protected Areas Unit of the World Conservation Monitoring Centre in Cambridge who has provided the latest available information on India's wildlife, and to Victoria Fletcher, also of the World Conservation Monitoring Centre.

GERALD CUBITT
GUY MOUNTFORT

This edition published in 2007 by
New Holland (Publishers) Ltd
London • Cape Town • Sydney • Auckland
www.newhollandpublishers.com

Garfield House, 86–88 Edgware Road, London, W2 2E, United Kingdom

80 McKenzie Street, Cape Town 8001, South Africa

Unit 1, 66 Gibbes Street, Chatswood, NSW 2067, Australia

218 Lake Road, Northcote, Auckland, New Zealand

ISBN 978 1 84537 923 0

Consultant Editor/additional text (1991 and 1998 editions): Michael Green
Preface and revised text (2007 edition): Hashim Tyabji
Designer: Joan Sutton; Jacket design: Phil Kay
Consultant Editor (2007 edition): James Parry
Assistant Editor (2007 edition): Giselle Osborne

Phototypeset by Hirt and Carter (Pty) Ltd/AKM Associates (UK) Ltd
Printed and bound in Singapore by Kyodo Printing Co (Singapore) Pte Ltd

FRONT COVER: Asian Elephants drinking in Kabini National Park (Lockwood & Dattatri/naturepl.com)
HALF TITLE: Adjutant Storks, Kaziranga National Park.
FRONTISPIECE: Great One-horned Rhinoceros, Royal Chitwan National Park, Nepal.
PAGE 5: Manas Tiger Reserve, Assam.
PAGE 8: Black-headed Ibis and chick.
PAGES 30/31: Sunset over the marshes at Keoladeo National Park, Rajasthan.
PAGE 36: Snow Leopard (Andy Rouse/NHPA)
PAGE 129: Black-necked Stork (Jean-Louis Le Moigne/NHPA)
PAGE 164: Asiatic Lion (E Hanumantha Rao/NHPA)

CONTENTS

PREFACE

It is now almost ten years since the last edition of this book was published, and several more since Guy Mountfort wrote his original introduction, which is retained in this new edition (with selected updates given in square brackets within the text). It is therefore an appropriate juncture at which to look back over the intervening period, particularly in view of the great changes currently underway in India in terms of economic growth and development. One aspect clearly stands out: the shocking transformation in the fortunes of India's most iconic animal, the tiger. A decade ago this was an animal whose future had apparently been secured by one of the world's most celebrated and successful conservation programmes in the shape of Project Tiger. Today the tiger in India (and, indeed, elsewhere) stands on the very brink of extinction in the wild, the victim of habitat destruction, poaching and incompetence in terms of conservation management.

A nationwide census conducted by the Wildlife Institute of India and provisionally declared at the end of May 2007 was predictably gloomy. Across Northern and Central India, the tiger population has fallen by over 60% since 2002, and the message is loud and clear – the tiger has disappeared from vast swathes of its former habitat, which meanwhile has been degraded and diminished by intensifying human pressure. The only meaningful numbers of tigers appear to be confined to tiger reserves and a few other protected areas, and the long-term viability of these populations is under threat as habitat degradation isolates them from other populations. For the first time since Project Tiger was launched in 1973, poaching seems to be taking a deadlier toll of tigers than habitat loss, and we are confronted by the once unthinkable prospect of losing the tiger ahead of its forest home. As we reflect upon this unfolding tragedy, a stark question presents itself, "If India cannot safeguard the tiger – the national animal and the main focus of its conservation efforts – what indeed can it hope to protect?"

Despite this disaster, it would be wrong to conclude that Indian wildlife conservation overall has lurched back thirty years. In many important respects the gains of the past three decades have become so deeply entrenched as to be virtually ineradicable. Chief amongst these is the widespread acceptance of the need for the conservation of wildlife and wilderness as an important priority of government. This is one of Indira Gandhi's most enduring legacies and was formulated at a time when most politicians across the developing world – including India – dismissed the whole conservation game as an unaffordable and eccentric luxury promoted by dilettante Westerners. In concrete terms this led to the Wildlife Protection Act (WLPA) of 1972, the formidable legal guarantor of India's biodiversity and the progenitor of Project Tiger (which by a 2006 amendment has been replaced by a potentially more effective National Tiger Conservation Authority).

Indeed, it is under the overarching shelter of the WLPA that the fascinating and diverse flora and fauna that constitute wild India have survived and enjoyed a tenuous prosperity in one of the world's most overcrowded countries. On the negative side however, the differences between 1972 and 2007 are profoundly sobering. Foremost is the doubling of the population from just over 500 million to over a billion in a country less than half the size of the United States of America – making India one of the most crowded places on Earth. The implications of this vastly increased pressure on land and resources – especially in a poor country – are self-evident.

Most significantly, the rural poor, who have hitherto borne the brunt of the cost of conservation – essentially subsidising the national effort by surrendering lands and resources for parks and protected areas while suffering loss of crops, livestock and, on occasion, their own lives, to wildlife – have found increasing political voice to secure their own well-being. As India's economy roars ahead, the aspirations of the forest-dwelling segment of the population rise in line with those of everyone else. And the present generation will no longer acquiesce to the bare subsistence levels that were the lot of their fathers. Aggravating the problems of land and resource hunger are significant failures of land use and agrarian policies that have locked people into a cycle of poverty, along with massive infrastructure projects that displace tens of thousands of people, either crowding them into decreasing parcels of open land or forcing them to illegally occupy forest land. It is, of course, an untenable situation. Tragically, the corrective measure, in the shape of the Tribal Forest Rights Act of 2006 (which gives forest dwellers far-reaching rights over forest lands and resources), is so extreme as to represent a grave long-term threat to the very survival of the Indian wilderness. One of its central premises is that traditional forest dwellers use forest resources sustainably, and have always been the best guardians of the forest. Perhaps this was true at a time when small human populations inhabited great swathes of forest, but with the situation now completely reversed it is a hopelessly unrealistic expectation.

For years wildlife managers in India and Nepal struggled to forge a formula of development that would reconcile the needs of wildlife with those of neighbouring human populations. This is the eco-development model that Guy Mountfort mentions in his original introduction. But over the years it has become abundantly clear that humans and wildlife – especially tigers – compete too closely for identical resources of land and protein to ever co-exist in a densely populated landscape. And with a population that is increasingly active politically, any Indian government – invariably constructed as a delicate coalition – needs to tread cautiously. Political will is therefore considerably compromised.

The situation is not totally bleak, however. While the era of top-down conservation is clearly over, the possibility has opened for a more durable and participatory conservation policy, to be fashioned from harnessing the great economic potential of wildlife tourism to the purpose of local development. India is well placed to tap this resource, with a large and prosperous middle class providing the bulk of visitors to the country's national parks. Together with international visitors, this constituency represents a rapidly growing potential asset for conservation, for as soon as wildlife becomes more valuable alive than dead, its long-term security is assured. Meanwhile, urgent action is required to save the tiger and the wilderness over which it presides. If India is to save the day it must not only enforce protection and prosecution, but also find the resolve to set aside enough of its land area exclusively for wildlife. Nothing else will suffice.

HashimTyabji
June 2007

A tiger in Kanha National Park, one of the last strongholds in India for this iconic species.

This book is dedicated to the memory of Shrimati Indira Gandhi, who throughout her long service as Prime Minister of India set a shining example to the world by her determination to protect the rich heritage of her country's wildlife.

FOREWORD

by HRH The Duke of Edinburgh KT, KG

Anyone concerned with the conservation of nature tends to be
obsessed with the disasters. There are plenty of conservation
disaster stories in India but, as this splendid book demonstrates
so beautifully, there are many success stories and much of her
superb natural heritage still survives.

I am sure that *Wild India* will give a great deal of pleasure for its
own sake but if ever a case had to be made for the conservation
of the world's natural heritage, it will be found most
persuasively in the pictures and text of this book.

INTRODUCTION

A traveller arriving by air almost invariably lands in the small hours of the night. When the doors open, a gust of heat like the blast from a furnace reminds him that this is India. The last time I landed at Dum-Dum, Calcutta's airport, at 2 a.m. the temperature stood at a clammy 33°C. In spite of the hour, the airport was swarming with people and every bench crowded to capacity with shrouded, sleeping figures and their cloth-bound bundles. Many lay untidily on the floor, still wearing their tinsel garlands of departure, but looking like the aftermath of a massacre. Until quite recently, airports in India, like railway stations, served as neighbourhood dormitories, through which travellers had to fight their way, aided by the enthusiastic khaki-clad baggage touts, who perhaps an hour later would triumphantly find their suitcases for them and obtain a taxi. Seasoned travellers will know that it is useless to hurry and that one after another the many officials, with contemplative devotion to duty, will examine minutely every stamp on every page of every passport. In planning an itinerary they will also have learned to accept at face value the charmingly worded notice stamped on the Indian Tourist Department brochure that 'all factual information is liable to change without notice'. What could be more disarmingly frank than this?

Whether you spend the remainder of the night in a modern hotel or in a mahogany and red velvet relic of the Victorian era, the unmistakable smell and sounds of India will greet the new day. The smell is compounded of burning cow-dung, spices and hot dust. From the roof-tops will come the squealing of Black Kites, locally called Pariahs for their scavenging habits, and as likely as not you will hear the chatter of the ubiquitous Mynahs. In the streets below there will be the incessant noise of taxi-horns and of people. Hundreds, thousands of them, some hurrying to work, others wandering aimlessly or talking in animated groups, or begging. In India it is almost impossible to escape the sight of people. Her population is increasing at a rate of something less than 2 per cent per annum and by the end of the 1990s it is estimated to have reached 1 billion (one thousand million) [by 2010 it is estimated to exceed 1.2 billion]. The city of Calcutta alone has a population of almost 12,000,000 – an average density of nearly 100,000 people to the square kilometre.

You can generalize about some countries, but not about India. It is a land of too many superlatives and contrasts, too great a range of differing scenes, too bewildering a complexity of ethnic origins, traditions, languages and religions. It is a beautiful land, whether seen in the glare of the midday sun when its colours are harshly brilliant, or at dawn when the palm trees stand like disembodied sentinels above the candescent mist rising from the paddyfields.

This fascinating region is so vast and its life so diverse that no one can know more than a fraction of it. In offering the reader something of the impression which it has made on me I am aware that it has been acquired, perhaps imperfectly, through Western eyes. The many photographs that follow, however beautiful in themselves, can represent only a fraction of the splendour which at every turn awaits the traveller. Because my interest and that of my colleague, the photographer Gerald Cubitt, lies primarily in the natural environment, we have deliberately omitted the incredibly rich heritage of man-made treasures, such as the voluptuous Hindu and assertively austere Islamic shrines, which for 3000 years have continued to increase in number. These are described and illustrated in a host of guide-books.

The India of the British Raj embraced not only the great Indian peninsula and its many princely States, but also what is now Pakistan to the west, Sikkim to the north and what is now Bangladesh in the east. To a certain extent its influence extended to Nepal and Bhutan. Sri Lanka (Ceylon) and even Myanmar (Burma), which has nothing in common with India, were usually included, if only because they were coloured pink on the map as being at that time within the British sphere of political influence. Since the Partition of India in 1947 all these countries have gained their independence

as Sovereign States, except Sikkim – which has become part of India.

Although this book deals principally with India, the phrase 'Indian subcontinent' is used when reference to these adjoining countries is also involved, for example in the case of the distribution of animal species or geological features. Sri Lanka is omitted because this great island has been separated from the continental land-mass for many millions of years.

Visitors to India may be confused by the disappearance of a few once-familiar place-names, because in 1956 the States were reorganized and many were given new names. For example, Bombay became officially 'Mumbai' in 1995; and on 1 October 1996 Madras became 'Channai'. India has the Hindi name Bharat, and although English is still the lingua franca of nearly all educated Indians, Hindi is officially the national language under the Constitution of India. However, since each ethnic group fiercely demands that its language should remain inviolate, it may be some years before this becomes fully effective. There would be an obvious unifying advantage in a single language. At present there are 18 'official' languages and 45 others spoken to a lesser degree. In addition, more than 700 quite different dialects are still current in various parts of the country. If ever a government had difficulty in communicating its policies to its people, it is that of India.

A crowded scene in Old Delhi. With a population of almost 950 million, India is enduring severe social and economic problems related to ever-growing human pressures.

The Legacies of Invasion

To understand the reasons for the extraordinary diversity of the Indian scene one must turn to its turbulent history and to the complex influences of its numerous religions. For 3000 years the renown of the rich natural resources of the subcontinent attracted powerful invaders, many of whom brought with them new religious beliefs which they established during their conquests. Indians often proudly claim to belong to the world's oldest civilization. It is certainly a very ancient one, though historical records before the Aryan invasion are vague. It probably dates back to the middle of the third millennium BC. Traces of Palaeolithic man exist, but evidence indicating a sequence of culture is lacking. The most important finds were made during excavations of the Bronze Age cities of Harappa and Mohenjo-Daro in the Indus valley. These suggest an occupation of about 600 years between 2500 and 1900 BC, by an agrarian Dravidian people – probably from Iran. Their strange pictographic alphabet and seals reveal a skilful craftsmanship superior to that of the Indo-Aryans. From their seals and figurines we learn that Tigers, Elephants and One-horned Rhinoceroses lived in the valley of the Indus, where today there is almost treeless desert. As no weapons were discovered in the excavations, these peaceable people were most probably exterminated by a more warlike tribe.

The first large-scale invasion of which records survive was that of the Aryans, who are thought to have come from central Asia. By 600 BC they had occupied all of northern India. Hinduism was already established, and here the Brahmins evolved classical Sanskrit. New religions were introduced with the teachings of Buddha and Mahavira. By the time of Alexander's short-lived invasion in 327 BC, northern India was ruled by the Mauryas. The rise of Emperor Ashoka in 274 BC saw the establishment of Buddhism throughout all of India except the extreme south. Under Ashoka, the first conservation measures were recorded and his Fifth Edict, protecting all wildlife except certain animals required for food, can still be read on the stone pillars on the boundaries of his empire. After his death, Buddhism began to decline and the Hindu religion to expand again, while India broke up into a number of small kingdoms.

Invasion by the Greeks, the Sakas, the Parthians and the Kushans followed in succession and these further enriched Indian culture. The Kushans did much to restore Buddhism. The third century AD witnessed a blossoming of the creative arts during the Gupta era, which was the golden age of Sanskrit literature, art, architecture, science and philosophy. But because of confusing dynastic rivalries during the following four centuries, India once more became fragmented and was unable to resist invasion by the White Huns and the powerful Arab legions. The subsequent long Moslem era was marked by widespread ruthless slaughter and pillage, which again changed the face of the country. By the beginning of the sixteenth century the Islamic faith had become established over a great part of India, although Hinduism remained the dominant religion.

The Moghul emperors who next ruled India were descendants of Tamerlane and the Mongol Genghiz Khan. The greatest of the Moghuls was undoubtedly Akbar, who ruled from 1556 to 1605. His administration was skilful and his treatment of Hindus conciliatory. [His successor, Jehangir, maintained his father's reforms whilst also furthering development of the arts and architecture. A keen and observant naturalist, and a gifted writer, his memoirs contain a wealth of information about animals and birds]. Shah Jehan, who followed him, introduced another period of literary progress and a programme of magnificent building, culminating in the treasured Taj Mahal at Agra as a monument to his wife, who had presented him with no fewer than 14 children. But the fabulous splendour of the Moghul court and the Peacock Throne hid some serious underlying weaknesses in the Mughal polity, and the opportunity for another attempted take-over was later seized, first by the Persians again, then by the Afghans and finally by the Marathas, who held power until 1761.

Meanwhile, covetous Western eyes had been turned towards the riches of India. First in the field were the Portuguese, who gained control of the Malabar coast. Next came the Dutch and the British and after them the French, the Danes and the Swedes. All the Western trading enterprises made treaties with various local Princes and fought one another in the scramble for advantage. Thanks to the power of its navy, Britain succeeded in excluding its competitors, and after many vicissitudes India became part of the British Empire in 1886. After the second World War, in which 2,000,000 Indian soldiers played a conspicuous part in all theatres, India finally gained independence in 1947 and proudly became a self-governing Republic. As Hindus and Moslems remained politically irreconcilable, Pakistan emerged as a separate Moslem nation. More recent history saw the transition of East Pakistan into independent Bangladesh.

Whatever the rights or wrongs of the long period of the British Raj, it bequeathed a legacy of lasting value in the form of an efficient civil service and a unifying network of roads and railways, to say nothing of many hospitals, schools and grandiose pseudo-Gothic civil buildings which still stand incongruously in Indian cities. (It also left a skilled forestry service – but the forestry practices it introduced are still being used today to deny basic rights to indigenous tribal populations.) Slavery, female infanticide and suttee (the burning of widows on their husbands' funeral pyres) had been firmly abolished.

The main religions of India, in numerical order of importance, are now those of the Hindus (comprising 82% of the population), the Moslems, the Christians, the Sikhs, the Buddhists, the Jains and the Zoroastrians. Within these sometimes strangely intermixed religions are many differing sects, particularly among Hindus. The bewildering Pantheon of Hindu gods and demons, many of which have alternative names, are worshipped at different times. Broadly speaking, they ensure reward for virtue in the next incarnation – and punishment for ill-doing. To a Hindu, God and Nature are one. No Hindu will willingly harm any animal, and the cow is regarded as sacred, as are certain other animals.

There is a considerable measure of animism in the more primitive forms of Hinduism. In Vedic theology all aspects of Nature have their own deities; thus Vayu rules the wind, Soma the plants, Garuda the birds, Jambavan the bears and so on. The elephant-headed, four-armed and pot-bellied god Ganesh must be propitiated before any important undertaking. The mythical Nagas, represented by a many-headed cobra, are the guardians of the underworld. All the Hindu poets and legends stress the moral imperative to regard Nature as beneficial to man.

The Jains are dissenters from Hinduism, and in its extreme form Jainism is a monastic order eschewing all material possessions. A strict Jain will kill no living thing and must keep his mouth covered in case his breath pollutes the air or harms flies. Moslems, on the other hand, safe in the knowledge that the Koran extols the virtues of the chase, are usually keen and skilful hunters. The fact that Hindus and Jains between them represent the great majority of the Indian population has undoubtedly been a major factor in maintaining the richness of Indian wildlife.

Geography and Climate

The roughly triangular Indian subcontinent is more than 3000 kilometres wide in the north and of similar length from the Himalayas to Cape Comorin, giving a total area of nearly 5,000,000 square kilometres, or roughly the size of Europe west of the USSR. It has three well-defined geographical regions – the Himalayan, the alluvial Indo-Gangetic Plain and the southern tableland of the Deccan. Each differs in appearance, languages and traditions.

It is generally recognized now that peninsular India was once part of the super-continent Gondwanaland, which included Africa, Antarctica, Madagascar, Australia and South America. Evidence of the link includes the remains of a primitive lizard, Lystrosaurus, found in South Africa, Antarctica, Bengal and China. As Gondwanaland broke up, India became separated and drifted across the globe on its molten crust, to crash slowly, but with titanic force, into Eurasia 40–50 million years ago. It extinguished the ancient Tethys Ocean, whose bed has been thrust up to 4000 metres in Tibet along the suture line of the Indian and Eurasian plates, just south of the Yarlung Zangbo river. Fossilized sea-shells such as ammonites can be seen here embedded in the sandstone and limestone rocks. These are now 800 kilometres from the nearest sea and 4 kilometres above the present sea level. The Indian plate has continued to thrust under Eurasia, and the Himalayas, which have risen in several great upheavals, are still rising at a rate of about a centimetre a year and moving northward at five centimetres a year. The height reached by the range in the late Pleistocene created a weather barrier which is responsible for India's monsoon climate.

The climate of the subcontinent is described as tropical monsoon, but it varies greatly and can offer extremes of heat and cold, total drought and torrential rain. In some areas not a drop of rain will fall for two years or more. Other regions may suddenly receive two years of average rainfall in only two days. Factors controlling these vagaries are the mountain ranges, the vastness of the exposed plain – extending for 2250 kilometres between the Indus and the Brahmaputra – and the extent of the long coastlines, which are exposed to the full force of the wind from both the Arabian Sea and the Indian Ocean. The western region – Pakistan, the Ranns of Kutch and the Rajasthan Desert – are dry and witheringly hot, the monsoon clouds passing over them but rarely releasing rain. In the east, monsoon rain is frequent, with an astonishing record of 10,870 millimetres one year in the Khasi Hills.

In the alluvial plain of the Ganges and Brahmaputra the monsoon rains pass regularly back and forth, depositing more than 2500 millimetres of water a year. India's capital, Delhi, gets a mere 730 millimetres or so, comparable to rainfall in England, but mainly between June and September. The peninsular region north of the Vindhya range has a fairly copious rainfall, while the plateau to the south usually receives its rain a month later. Cyclones accompanied by tidal waves periodically devastate the coasts of the Bay of Bengal, with horrifying loss of life.

In 1988, the most serious floods on record caused damage spread over more than half the country's total area. But in general terms the Indian weather is cool in January and February and hot from March to May, with the monsoon advancing from June to October and retreating again in November and December. The first quarter of the year is usually delightful, with brilliant sunshine and only modest heat recalling a Mediterranean summer.

Vegetation and the Monsoon

The subcontinent is extremely rich in plants with an estimated 15,000 vascular species. About one-third of India's flowering plant species are endemic. A large number of species originate from the surrounding countries. European and Siberian origins are obvious in the coniferous trees of the Himalayas. In the western half are Deodars, Long-leafed Pines, Western Himalayan Firs and Bhutan Cypresses. In the more tropical eastern half these are replaced by other local varieties of Spruce, Larch, Hemlock, Pine and Fir. The thorny xerophytic vegetation of the Pakistan and Rajasthan deserts much resembles that of Arabia and the Middle East, while that of the southern peninsula has fairly obvious Malaysian affinities, with a smaller admixture of East African.

In the humid Gangetic Plain the native Sal forests are the

mainstay of the timber industry. Teak, an important quick-growing commercial species, is cultivated chiefly in areas of high rainfall in the east and south. The commercial crops of the subcontinent are rice and other cereals, tea, coffee, sugar cane, rubber, cotton, jute, oilseed and an abundance of fruits, nuts and spices. Further variety in the vegetation has resulted from countless deliberate introductions from other continents. Including these, the number of tree species alone is now about 1200, many of which have spectacular blossoms and have become naturalized in the wild.

The most common and one of the most beautiful Indian trees is the Cassia, or Indian Laburnum, which produces masses of drooping bunches of yellow flowers, followed by dangling seed-pods 60 centimetres long. In coastal regions the Indian Coral Tree is equally colourful, with spikes of bright coral-red flowers. Because of its hard wood it is frequently used for fencing, and when the wood is fresh the posts readily take root to produce new wayside trees. Many city streets are lined with Queen's Flower, the purple blossoms of which fall to carpet the pavements. Another

widespread and economically important tree is the Makua, the flowers of which are used in the making of liquor.

One of the introduced species is the Baobab, which has a grotesque bulbous trunk and was brought in from Africa many centuries ago by Moslem traders. The Gulmohar (Flamboyant) came from Madagascar and is now perhaps the most common urban tree. Its abundant orange-red flowers, produced in February when it is bare of leaves, and its later feathery foliage brighten many a city park, as do the scarlet bells of the Tulip Tree. The various Eucalypts came from Australia and Tasmania, the Sandalwood from Indonesia, while the Jacarandas, with their beautiful lilac-blue flowers, originated in Brazil.

The Flame of the Forest, which flowers at the beginning of the hot season, is another widespread and spectacular species, with orange-red blossoms. The extravagantly flowering Silk Cotton was known in the earliest Indian mythology as the tree beneath which Pitamaha, the creator of the world, rested after his labours. It is one of the best shade-trees and produces large red flowers, the calyx of which is eaten as a delicacy. The cotton dropping from its fat seedpods blankets the surroundings, and is harvested for stuffing mattresses. The sharp conical spines on its bark deter anyone from climbing it, but despite this, a friend of mine was once obliged to climb a Silk Cotton at high speed when treed by a Tigress, only to find that it housed a colony of savagely biting tree-ants, to which he had to submit for half an hour before the Tigress withdrew.

My favourites among the flowering trees are the various Bauhinias, with their large mauve, pink or white single blossoms. The Climbing Bauhinias are almost as beautiful, their masses of creamy-white flowers cascading down from hundreds of great trees in the foothills of the Himalayas and in the forests of the Western Ghats.

Two trees have important religious significance in India. One,

Seasonal changes from the dry season to the wet season produce very pronounced results, as shown by these views of a lake in the Ranthambore National Park.

indigenous in the sub-Himalayan region, is the Banyan; the other is the Peepal. Both members of the numerous fig family, these trees are characterized by powerful and invasive growth. If planted near buildings, they easily demolish them. They are very long-lived. The Banyan increases by roots descending from the branches, so that they spread over an astonishingly large area. A venerable tree at least 500 years old dominates a sacred grove near Avantpur in Andhra Pradesh. With more than 1100 prop roots it covers an area of 2.1 hectares and is now recognized as the largest example of its species. Villagers venerate both species and make use of the extensive shelter they provide as community centres. The Buddha is said to have achieved enlightenment while meditating under a Peepal, and both Hindus and Buddhists hold religious ceremonies beneath these trees, which they often believe to be female Banyans.

One such tree is said to be 2150 years old, although the evidence for this is somewhat doubtful.

Among the most frequently seen palm trees are the Palmyra or Toddy Palk, the Coconut, the Sago, the Wild Date and the Betel Nut. The red, expectorated juice of chewed Betel Nut stains the ground in every Indian town and village. According to Indian doctors, the juice is one of the major causes of mouth cancer. In the Mangrove swamps the channels are often fringed with graceful, short-stemmed Nipa Palks, which are the mainstay of the Bengali thatching industry.

Botanists divide the vegetation of the subcontinent into 16 distinct types, ranging from tropical wet evergreen, semi-evergreen and moist deciduous to dry alpine scrub. Each has distinctive communities of dependent wildlife. The vegetation and indeed all forms of life, including man, are governed by the power and vagaries of the monsoon. The rains are seldom predictable. In some years and in some regions the monsoon capriciously fails, and there is widespread drought and famine. Wells run dry over huge areas and, where water remains, it is measured by the halfcupful. The lesson of the imbalance of Nature is a harsh one. Equally capriciously, the volume of monsoon rainfall in India may be so great that rivers rise by as much as 32 metres, drowning hundreds of villages and causing great tracts of soil and vegetation, including large trees, to slide down mountain slopes and demolish roads and railways. Despite dams and barrages, such catastrophes are frequent, and the loss of life is horrific. In 1983 more than 800 people were drowned in Gujarat State alone, while 1000 were drowned elsewhere in India. Every year, hundreds of millions of tons of valuable top-soil are carried down the rivers and into the sea, where new islands are created by the accumulated silt. One such island appeared off the mouth of the Ganges a few years ago, and is already more than 16 kilometres wide. Charts are of little value near the river mouth because of the constantly changing contours of the sea floor caused by the discharge of silt.

The sheer violence and duration of monsoon rainfall as experienced in north-east India and Myanmar (Burma) has to be seen to be believed. The most torrential European rain is by comparison a mere shower. Nevertheless, it is the life-blood of the subcontinent. When the monsoon breaks, the villagers rejoice and give thanks to the god Varuna, the controller of the waters of life. The starving domestic buffaloes run bellowing to the village ponds, which for months have been mere sun-cracked depressions, to wallow with only their eyes and noses above the longed-for water. Were it not for the cushioning effect of the dense forests in the mountains and hills, the north-eastern parts of India would long since have lost most of their essential top-soil. There is clear evidence of this in areas which have been clear-felled to make way for the expansion of human settlements; instead of rich and varied forest there is now a semi-desert of exposed laterite subsoil.

Both vegetation and bird life in India are largely controlled by the incidence of the monsoon. Many trees and plants which provide fruit bear crops twice a year in conformity with the monsoon cycle. The migration and nesting of most birds also conform, so that advantage can be taken of the abundance of insect life and fresh vegetation which follows. Certain migratory birds are regarded by farmers as infallible heralds of the rain – for example, the Rain Quail, the Koel and Pied Cuckoo. Western farmers may smile at this, but in India the accuracy of the movement of migratory birds in relation to the rains and the abundance of food is not to be scoffed at.

Three regions are world famous among botanists – Kashmir, Nepal and Bhutan. The higher reaches of Kashmir and the Nepalese Himalayas provided many of the most beautiful alpine flowers which now grow in our gardens, while from Bhutan and Sikkim originated a large percentage of our cultivated orchids and greenhouse plants. For Rhododendrons and Azaleas, the area between the Khumbu and Mount Khangchendzonga on the border of Sikkim one can see a staggering variety of species and such a combination of massed colours as to render anyone speechless.

In Sikkim, Bhutan and parts of North Bengal and Assam one can still see the true richness of the jungle of the Himalyan foothills. Further south, in the Chittagong Hill Tracts of Bangladesh, there are still some large areas of unspoilt tropical wet evergreen forest in all its exuberance of impenetrable cane thickets, creeping bamboos,

bromeliads and flowering epiphytes. Around clearings and along river banks huge hanging curtains of invasive Mikania vines and other creepers hang from the trees, their blossoms swarming with Sunbirds, White-eyes and Flowerpeckers. The abundant fruits of the climbing figs are constantly consumed by various species of monkeys, green and pink pigeons and Hornbills. Exploring this region in 1966, I came across a tragic example of engineering miscalculation. At the Kaptai Dam, thousands of hectares of ancient and magnificent forest had been needlessly drowned in 1963 because someone had mistaken the ultimate level to which the water would rise. Regiments of the giant tree skeletons standing in the lake were all that remained of an area where once wild Elephants lived in the Pablakhali Wildlife Sanctuary.

In the northern and eastern plains of India, at around the 1000 metre level, a very different type of much more open forest occurs – the Sal forest, where the beautiful Sal is the dominant species. Perhaps the most famous and still largely unspoilt tracts of Sal are in the Siwalik foothills and in the Kanha National Park in Madhya Pradesh. In the lower Indo-Gangetic plain the scene again changes – to patches of tropical dry deciduous forest rising to only about 23 metres, with a light undergrowth of shrubs and grasses. Man's hand lies heavy on this region, and most of the trees are constantly lopped for firewood. Grazing cattle are everywhere, compounding the problem. Further south in the Deccan plateau and east of the Western Ghats there is thorn forest. The once extensive thorn forests of the Indus valley in Pakistan have long since been destroyed. Much of north-western India, where there is very little rainfall, is now either desert or has scattered patches of stunted Acacias and other drought-tolerant species. In the Thar Desert, a single plant species, *Prosopis juliflora*, provides almost the only fuel available to villagers and the only fodder for their cattle.

Finally, in the tidal creeks in the Sundarbans delta, the vegetation is again completely different, a closed evergreen tidal forest of some 20 species of mangrove trees, with an undergrowth of Pandanus Screw Palms, canes and other salt-tolerant shrubs.

The forests of north-east India, like those on the seaward side of the Western Ghats and in the Hill Tracts, are broadly classified as monsoon forests. Most visitors are deterred from exploring them because their margins alongside the occasional roads or rivers are usually walled in by a twisted mass of huge, sun-loving vines which are penetrable only by slashing a way through. The effort, however, is well worthwhile. Once beneath the high closed canopy, which is often 45–60 metres above ground, progress is relatively easy, little vegetation being able to grow in the gloom of the forest floor. The air is noticeably stagnant and humid and only occasional sparkles of sunlight can penetrate. The trees are of bewildering variety; as many as 100 different species have been identified within an area of one hectare. A single tree may be host to 500 different species of beetles. Some of the giant tree trunks, such as the Kapoks, have wide buttresses, others grow from a pyramid of stilt-roots. Here are there an immense strangling fig has wrapped its web of climbers around a big tree and killed it in the struggle to reach the sunlight far above. Other trees rise straight and magnificent, without branching until 30 metres above ground. Some of these giants have silvery-white bark, heightening the impression that you are walking in the nave of a dimly-lit cathedral. The litter on the forest floor teems with grotesquely formed insects and colourful fungi, all busily engaged in helping the myriads of unseen micro-organisms to break down the rotting leaves and fallen trees to provide the soil nutrients on which the forest lives. Decomposition is ten times more rapid than in a temperate forest. A tropical forest is never silent. By day there is the constant hum of flies, bees, wasps and hornets and by night the loud rasping chorus of countless cicadas and frogs.

There is little visible movement at ground level in a rain forest, except for the occasional passing of a sounder of Wild Boar or a solitary Mouse Deer, but in the leaf canopy above there is a constant coming and going of monkeys, squirrels and birds, all feasting on the plentiful fruit, nectar or tender leaves. Stand still for a few moments and watch the ground, and you will see the ever-hungry leeches approaching from all around, looping their sinister way with uncanny skill to the potential source of mammalian blood. A huge percentage of the billions of leeches which inhabit rain forests never succeed in getting a meal during their short lives.

The complex aerial roots of the Banyan tree.

Any passing mammal is therefore an immediate victim. They drop in hundreds from the vegetation, alerted by the vibration of footsteps and attracted by body-heat. It is almost impossible to escape their attention, and the speed with which they penetrate clothing and even the lace-holes in boots is astonishing. They are, however, easily removed with the aid of a lighted cigarette or a pinch of salt. If merely brushed off, they usually leave their suckers behind - the wound then bleeds for a long time because of the anti-coagulant they exude, and it may become a tiresome sore. However, it is possible to get used to the leeches, and they are a small price to pay for seeing the many marvels of the rain forest.

There are many different kinds of rain forest in the equatorial regions of the world. All the various types are, alas, now disappearing before their scientific secrets or their potential values to man have been fully ascertained. The world's tropical moist forests are being cleared at an estimated 26 hectares per minute. It is predicted that the rate of deforestation will decline, but, nevertheless, by 2020 the total area under tropical forest will have diminished by 10 to 20 per cent. In the case of India, the annual rate of deforestation (i.e. complete destruction of forest cover) is estimated to have been 3,400 square kilometres during the 1980s.

The Riches of Wildlife

The wildlife of the Indian subcontinent, like its vegetation, emphasises by its diversity of species the widely differing habitats and available climatic zones . There are some 365 species of different mammals, about 1260 species of birds, over 400 species of reptiles and about 180 species of amphibians. By comparison with Africa, however, the larger animals are more difficult to see, most of them living not out in open savanna as in Africa, but in forests.

India was one of the very few countries whose Prime Minister for a number of decades had a very strong personal interest in the conservation of wildlife. Unfortunately, however, the late Mrs Gandhi was unable to prevent the inexorable impact of Man on the natural environment. Nevertheless, the wise conservation policies which she introduced did much to reduce this impact and raise the level of conservation awareness among policy- and decision-makers. At the time of the British Raj, all the many books written by soldiers and government officials, most of whom were also hunters, gave the impression that game animals proliferated in such numbers as to seem inexhaustible. Certainly the great hunting parties organized by the Maharajahs in honour of local or visiting dignitaries suggested this by the quantities which they slaughtered

year after year. One such example was a shikar which in a few days in 1919 accounted for 120 Tigers, 27 Leopards and 18 Sloth Bears. Many Englishmen claimed to have shot 100 Tigers during their tours of duty in India. A few hunters claimed as many as 300, the record being held by the Maharajah of Surguja, who is on record as having declared that during his lifetime he had killed no fewer than 1150 of these animals. Many Maharajahs claimed their first Tiger at the tender age of twelve and continued shooting them until well into their seventies.

Tigers had been hunted even before the Indo-Aryans arrived in the Indus valley. The earlier Bronze Age Harappa civilization used the image of a Tiger on its seals, and the first Moghuls are known to have enjoyed Tiger-hunting. It became the sport of kings and remained so for more than a thousand years. The dangerous pastime of hunting on foot with spears or bows and arrows gave the Tiger at least an even break. It was not until the invention of the matchlock gun in the fifteenth century that their odds began to shorten. By the seventeenth century, with the introduction of the flintlock and rifled barrel, they swung heavily against the Tiger and all other game animals. No animals stand a chance of survival against modern high-velocity rifles with telescopic sights. It was not hunting, however, which was the principal cause of the decline of wildlife in the subcontinent, but the progressive destruction of the forests where most of the animals lived.

Not until the late 1930s was the first voice raised in defence of the Tiger, when the great hunter-naturalist Jim Corbett published articles expressing concern about their declining population. He prophesied, to the astonishment of many, that unless excessive hunting and the destruction of forests could be curbed, the Tiger would soon become extinct. Few believed him, because at that time it was thought that there were still at least 40,000 Tigers in India, to say nothing of those in the adjacent countries. This figure was, however, mere guesswork.

After the Partition of India and the turmoil which followed it, little thought was given to the subject. Law and order had broken down and villagers, who in the past had participated in hunting only as hired beaters, now had access not only to guns but also to the previously protected forests and hunting reserves. Tigers and other game animals were shot, trapped and poisoned everywhere and a thriving black market in skins was soon created. By the time law and order were re-established, it was several years before these practices could be brought under control. The process was not helped by the fact that, as soon as it was realized that Tigers were rapidly disappearing, hunters from all over the world hurried to India to bag one before it was too late. Tiger-skin rugs and coats were by then selling in New York, Paris and Tokyo for as much as $5,000, and commercially sponsored hunting and smuggling became big business.

Meanwhile, the rapidly increasing human population, dizzy with the euphoria of Independence, was clamouring for land. The plains were already over-populated and the obvious solution was to exploit the protected forests, many of which had been owned by the now dispossessed Maharajahs. The speed with which forests disappeared in the following 30 years, not only in India but also throughout Asia, was accelerated by the world-wide demand for timber, which provided much-needed hard currency to the exporting countries. The effect on wildlife was devastating.

Tigers are essentially animals of the forest, as are their prey – the Wild Boar and deer. Once deprived of their habitat they are doomed. The Indian Government, through the State Forest and Wildlife Departments, and encouraged by the Indian Board for Wild Life and the World Wide Fund for Nature (WWF - then known as the World Wildlife Fund), conducted a census in 1972 which revealed that only about 1827 Tigers survived in India. In Nepal, Sikkim, Bhutan, Bangladesh and western Myanmar (Burma), where the Indian race of the Tiger also occurs, there were perhaps a further 600–700. Throughout Asia, where the other seven races or subspecies occurred, a similarly catastrophic decline had been caused. The Caspian and Balinese races were already extinct. Only five Javan Tigers remained, only about 300 Siberian in the USSR and northern China and perhaps 500-1000 Sumatran. The Chinese race, by government edict, had been almost exterminated as 'harmful to agricultural and pastoral progress'. The Indo-Chinese, which had a huge range from eastern Myanmar (Burma) to the China Sea, was thought to number about 2000. Thus a dominant animal species which in the 1930s had a probable total population in Asia of about 100,000, had dwindled in only 40 years to a mere 5000 or so. It was obvious that at such a rate of decline the Tiger would be totally extinct everywhere within a very few years.

The Tiger has always been my favourite animal, and I have studied its behaviour in the wild in four countries. It is also one of the world's most magnificent and best known animals. I therefore became closely involved in the international campaign which the World Wide Fund for Nature launched in 1971 to save it from extinction. The response was immediate and gratifying, nearly $2 million being subscribed by the public, world-wide. Thanks to the willing co-operation of a dozen countries in Asia, including the USSR and China (but not Myanmar (Burma)), the Tiger was given legal protection and soon provided with more than 40 protected reserves. Under the Convention on the International Trade in Endangered Species, the export and import of Tiger skins was banned and their hunting was either banned or strictly controlled.

Operation Tiger, as the campaign was called, began in India, where the late Prime Minister, Mrs Indira Gandhi, set an example of government initiative which inspired the rest of Asia. Her interest in wildlife, inspired by her father Pandit Jawaharlal Nehru, was very real, and she made the Tiger the symbol of India's dedication to the preservation of all wildlife. In return for the promise of technical equipment and scientific assistance to the value of $1 million from the Word Wide Fund for Nature, the Indian Government launched its own Project Tiger in 1973, and has since created 23 [now 28] Tiger reserves within a total area of 31,000 [now 37,761] square kilometres. Moreover, the states have sustained a loss of many millions of dollars in revenue from logging operations curtailed within reserve borders. Money for Project Tiger has been used on training, equipping and housing guards, on building patrol roads, on improving water resources and fire control, on trans-locating vulnerable villages and on the management of the forests and grazing areas. Because the planning was on the basis of improving the entire ecosystem, not only the Tigers and their prey species benefited, but also all the mammals, birds, reptiles, insects and vegetation. Another important outcome of skilled management has been that many previously seasonal streams in the reserves now flow perennially, to the benefit of the surrounding villages as well as the wildlife.

By 1989 the tiger population was considered to be thriving once more, having increased from an estimated 1,800 at the beginning of Project Tiger to some 4,300 [but in recent years the situation has changed again, see *Preface*]. Their value as a tourist attraction has been recognized. Now accustomed to the sight of tourists on elephants, they can even be seen in daylight in reserves such as Kanha and the Royal Chitwan National Park in Nepal. The excellently equipped 'Tiger Tops' lodge in Chitwan, with its well trained guides and riding elephants, has become internationally famous, and tourists are also flocking to the Indian Tiger reserves.

Project Tiger had its opponents among the *shikar* organizers and outfitters, who saw their livelihood threatened; Tiger hunting used to be a lucrative business and wealthy Americans were prepared to pay as much as $20,000 for the privilege of killing a single animal. A more understandable opposition arose because of a sudden steep increase in the number of villagers killed by Tigers. Among the worst incidents were in the North Kheri region near the Dudwa National Park, where in five years no fewer than 95 people are said to have been killed. Such an outbreak was obviously a very serious matter. Not unexpectedly, the shikar outfitters made capital of it and demanded a return to Tiger hunting. However, the then Director of Project Tiger, Mr H.S. Panwar, refused to be panicked into taking precipitate action. Instead, he examined in detail the circumstances of each attack and concluded that most deaths arose from accidental confrontations, in which the Tiger made a defensive attack. The problem was attributed to the peripheral buffer zone of savanna being replaced by sugar cane plantations right to the edge of the Tiger reserve. These plantations provided good cover for Tigers to rest during the heat of the day and thereby increased the likelihood of direct encounters with villagers. This tragic experience clearly demonstrated the importance of the original plan to establish and maintain buffer zones around Tiger reserves for the benefit of both the Tiger and villagers.

Tigers are not inherent man-killers and in normal circumstances go out of their way to avoid humans. I have never carried a gun when studying them, even on foot, except once when in an area of known man-eaters and even then had no cause to use it. In the majority of instances when they have been shot for attacking men it has been found that they did so because they were either starving, or were incapable of hunting their normal prey because of infirmity, shot-gun wounds or loss of teeth. Outbreaks of man killing rarely occur where ungulates, such as Wild Boar and deer, are sufficient to meet their food requirements and where the habitat remains intact. In some parts of India, tribal people have lived for centuries in forests where Tigers were numerous. In fact, the tribal villagers are so casual about seeing them that they give them nicknames and make them keep their distance merely by shouting or beating tin cans. Neither side attempts to take over the territory of the other and they share the forest in watchful harmony.

Overall, Project Tiger has been successful of achieving its primary objective of conserving the Tiger; not only was the decline arrested, but reversed. However, poaching for the tiger bone trade has become rampant and widespread during the 1990s and by 1993 the Tiger population was officially estimated to be 3,750. According to the present Director of Project Tiger, Mr P.K. Ken, India has been losing 200-300 Tigers annually to poachers since 1989 and the population may now total only 3,000 or fewer [but see *Preface*].

Control has been lost over several Tiger reserves, sometimes as a direct result of political militant groups using them as refuges, as in the case of the Bodos in Manas, Assam. Most Tiger reserves are subject to illegal grazing and tree felling, and all suffer from the antagonism of people living just outside their borders. Increasingly, it is recognised that the resource needs of such local people must be met through an integrated and participatory approach to management in order for biodiversity to be effectively conserved within the reserves.

In September 1997, the Prime Minister of India, Inder Kumar Gujral, announced that his government was considering reforms to the mechanisms that govern India's wildlife "to ensure the safety of the tiger and the natural heritage of our nation." This announcement followed immediately after a meeting of the Project

Signboard at the entrance to Bandipur Tiger Reserve.

Tiger Steering Committee at which a number of far reaching decisions were taken, including: immediate increase of funds for Project Tiger and initiation of new mechanisms to transmit funds directly to Tiger reserves; lifting the ban on recruitment of personnel to Project Tiger and filling the 40% of posts currently vacant on a priority basis; creation of a new cell to deal exclusively with the illegal trade in wildlife; cessation or reduction of all negative development activities in and around Tiger reserves; declaration of new areas under Project Tiger; and identification of corridors to link important Tiger habitats and ensure their future viability. The Committee has also recommended the establishment of a Tiger Authority of India, believing this to be the most effective means of effectively and rapidly introducing such changes [A National Tiger Conservation Authority has now been created]. These developments are truly remarkable and the conservation community, and world at large, now waits to see if the present government, under a somewhat shaky coalition, has the commitment and clout to deliver these promises.

A small remnant population of Asiatic Lions still survives in the Gir National Park and Sanctuary in the Indian State of Gujarat. They closely resemble the African Lion from which they originated, though the males usually have somewhat less heavy manes. I am inclined to agree with the late E. P. Gee that this is probably not a natural evolutionary change but the result of selective hunting – the hunter always choosing the animal with the biggest mane. The range of the Asiatic Lion once extended from Greece through the Middle East to central India, but when I first visited the Gir in 1969 their world population stood at only 177 and was declining. The Gir forest had been the property of the local Moslem rulers, the Nawabs of Junagadh, who had protected the Lions since early in this century. When the last Nawab fled to Pakistan after the Partition of India, his land was speedily over-run by villagers and their cattle. Nearly all the deer had vanished and the Lions were obliged to feed on the thousands of domestic cattle, which were rapidly destroying the vegetation. Whenever Lions killed a cow, the Harijans (the so-called 'untouchables', who alone will dispose of dead animals) seized the carcass in order to sell the meat, bones and hide. The Lions seldom got a square meal and were starving.

Dr Paul Joslin and I made independent studies of the Gir and I sent our recommendations to Mrs Gandhi. Thanks to her intervention and the efforts of the Gujarat State government, the Gir National Park was put under skilled management and has since become one of the best managed protected areas in India. Nearly all the local graziers and some 20,000 cattle have successfully been resettled beyond its boundaries. With the recovery of the grazing areas, the population of various deer species reached an astonishing level of 11,000 animals, providing the Lions with an abundance of their natural prey. The Lion population has continued to increase from about 100 adults in 1979 through 191 adults in 1985 to 221 adults in 1990. In 1996 the total number of lions increased to 304. A further 30–40 lions live in the agricultural mosaic periphery to the national park and sanctuary.

Sundarbans Tiger Reserve faces a problem with man-eating tigers which, over the years, have exacted a heavy toll from Bengali honey gatherers, wood-cutters and fishermen. To combat this situation, the Director of the reserve devised wooden effigies of human figures draped in dhotis and bearing a human scent. The figures are then wrapped with electrified wire and placed in selected positions in the mangrove forest. When a tiger attacks the figure, it receives a severe shock. Project Tiger staff are optimistic that this technique will soon prove an effective deterrent to tigers that attack humans.

Unfortunately, the once abundant Cheetahs, of which some thousands of the Asiatic race used to be kept by the Mughals for hunting Chinkara Gazelles and Blackbuck, are now extinct in Asia, except for a very few in Iran. The last apparently wild Cheetah in India was shot in 1947. The possibility of reintroducing the species by transfer from the small surviving Iranian population is now being considered, but I fear that the number available may be too small to justify the experiment.

The three leopard species, however, still survive, but only the common Leopard, which is a particularly adaptable creature, has maintained its original range. It is most commonly encountered near villages, where it preys on dogs, goats, sheep, calves and poultry. Usually called the Panther in India, it not infrequently occurs in an all-black form, through which the typical 'rosette' markings are still visible in sunlight. The so-called Black Panther is not, however, a true species by a morph, or colour phase, of the Leopard. Its relative, the beautiful Snow Leopard, continues to be shot and trapped in some parts of the Himalayas for the value of its magnificent fur, which is creamy-white with large dark rosettes. Living near the snow-line, it preys on Marmots, Mountain Hares and the various mountain sheep and goats, as well as livestock. In order to maintain a firm grip on ice it has evolved hairy soles to its feet. Probably the largest surviving population is in the Jigme Dorji National Park created by H M King Jigme Singye Wangchuk of Bhutan adjacent to the international border with Tibet. Other important protected areas for Snow Leopards include Pakistan's Khunjerab National Park, Hemis and Nanda Devi national parks in India, and Shey-Phoksundo National Park in Nepal. Clouded Leopards, by contrast, are strictly arboreal tropical species, whose range is from southern Nepal eastward to China. Because of their short legs and very long canine teeth they have been likened to miniature Sabre-toothed Tigers, but these prehistoric beasts were not their ancestors. Their greyish-buff coats are heavily mottled with blackish blotches and they have abnormally long tails. With luck they can still be seen in north-eastern India, Nepal, Bhutan and the Chittagong Hill Tracts.

Intermediate in size between the leopards and the smaller cats is the very attractive Golden Cat, which is well over a metre in length and with its unmarked tawny coat resembles a miniature Puma. It is said to occur in Assam, Nepal, Sikkim and the Chittagong Hill Tracts eastward through Myanmar (Burma) and Malaysia.

Of the six seven cats, one, the strikingly long-haired Pallas's Cat of Tibet and Ladakh, is rarely seen, though skins appear occasionally in native markets. It has a distinctly flattened head and ears and hunts small rodents on high, rocky ground. Desert Cats and Jungle Cats are still fairly numerous in north-west to central India and in parts of Pakistan. Both have sandy coloration, the Jungle Cat being easily distinguished by its shorter, banded tail. The Desert Cat has hairy soles to its feet, enabling it to move swiftly in soft sand. The largest of the group is the Fishing Cat, which has a rough, greyish-tawny coat with rows of diffuse dark streaks and rather short legs. It is found chiefly in reed-beds and jungle in the Indo-Gangetic Plain, Orissa, the Malabar coast and the Indus delta in Pakistan. Like a domestic cat at a goldfish bowl it catches fish with a lightning-quick scoop of its semi-webbed paw. It swims strongly and, unlike other cats, also dives occasionally. The Rusty-spotted Cat is found throughout western and central India. Two other species, the pale buff, round-spotted Leopard Cat and the more heavily blotched Marbled Cat, which resembles a miniature Clouded Leopard in its markings, inhabit the Himalayan forests. A few of the former are also found in southern India, while the latter is chiefly restricted to the north-east. All, although now legally protected, are heavily exploited by poachers for their beautifully marked skins. A study by the World Wide Fund for Nature and the Zoological Survey of India has drawn attention to the need to protect the habitats of all the small cats if they are to survive.

Two much larger felines are the Lynx and the Caracal. With their sandy coloration and upstanding tufted ears they are easily recognized. The former, which is a race of the European Lynx, is the larger of the two and is heavily built, with a very short, black-tipped tail. Occupying the highlands of Gilgit, Ladakh and Tibet up to an altitude of 3000 metres, it preys on birds, hares, rodents and occasionally wild sheep and goats. The more slender, longer-tailed

Caracal inhabits the desert regions of Pakistan and India. It is a more agile hunter, sometimes killing even such fleet-footed creatures as Chinkara Gazelles. I once saw one stalk a flock of sandgrouse drinking at a water-hole, two of which it killed in a whirlwind attack. Caraclas used to be trained to hunt bustards and peafowl, but have now become rather rare.

There are three bear species in the Indian region, the Brown Bear, the Himalayan Black bear and the Sloth Bear. All three are formidable animals which are frequently in conflict with man and are therefore often shot. The range of the Brown Bear is only just within the region, at high altitudes throughout the Himalayas. If food is scarce, it plays havoc with domestic flocks, although its usual diet is fruit, roots and rodents. The Black Bear is still fairly numerous in the Himalayas, occasionally as high as the tree-line but more often at lower altitudes. Occasionally a vagrant wanders as far south as Sylhet. Its footprints in the snow, with five clearly defined toes, are rather like those of a man, though the long claw-marks are easily distinguished. When the melting snow obliterates the claw-marks, the probable origin of the mythical Yeti remains for all to see. The Sherpas of Nepal are firm believers in the Yeti, but the remains of one exhibited in a Buddhist monastery have been proved to be an unconvincing fake.

Black Bears hibernate during the coldest part of the winter, in leaf-lined rock or earth caves. When they descend to the foothills in search of fruit they are frequently disturbed by woodcutters and farmers, whom they attack without hesitation if cornered. The late

A Jungle Cat in Ranthambore National Park.

Dr Robert Fleming, a famous authority on Himalayan birds who at that time was a surgeon at the Kathmandu hospital, told me of scores of men brought to him with terrible wounds caused by the raking claws of Black Bears and that many had been hugged and bitten in the face.

The smaller Sloth Bear has much more shaggy and greyer fur than the Black, giving it a distinctly untidy appearance. It has a whitish 'V' on its chest, but this is less obvious than on the shining fur of the Black Bear. Its grey snout is disproportionately long, and when it is ambling along in its forest habitat it always strikes me as a rather ungainly caricature of its handsome relative. Feeding chiefly on fruit and insects, it also searches diligently for honey, climbing the highest branches for the hanging combs of wild bees, which, if it cannot reach them, it shakes down with great vigour. Sure signs that a Sloth Bear is about are the devastated termite mounds which it excavates and the huge pits which it digs in search of grubs. Orchards and plantations of sugar-cane are often raided, but humans are seldom attacked. One of the best places to see these animals is in the Royal Chitwan National Park in Nepal, when the new grass is just emerging and they are hunting in daylight for termite nests. Later, when the grass is high, they are more likely to be in dense forest, feeding on mangoes and wild figs. Dumkhal and Ratanmahal in Gujarat were created sanctuaries specifically to protect the Sloth Bear.

After the bears, it is inevitable to think next of the Red Panda, which also inhabits the Himalayan forests eastward across Asia.

Pandas, however, are not bears, their closest relatives being probably the North American racoons. The range of the Giant Panda of China does not extend to India, but its much smaller relation, the Red Panda, can be seen in the temperate forests of Nepal, Sikkim and Bhutan, from about 2400 to 3800 metres where bamboo, its main food plant, is abundant.

The Asian Elephant is a familiar sight as a domesticated animal throughout south-east Asia. It is slightly smaller than its African counterpart and easily distinguished by its smaller ears and rounded, rather than hollow, back. Its hind feet have four nails instead of the African's three and its trunk only a single 'lip'. The cows usually lack tusks and those of the bulls are seldom very large. Being forest animals, elephants have suffered, like so many other species, from the relentless destruction of their habitat. Some 38,000 to 51,000 Asian Elephants are believed to survive in the wild., with India thought to have the largest number [in 2002 the population was estimated at 27,000]. Some herds in the north-west of the country move into Nepal, while others in the north-east are shared with Bhutan. Another 200 to 350 elephants are found in the Chittagong Hills of Bangladesh, some of which move into India or Myanmar (Burma). Everywhere their numbers are declining.

Domesticated elephants are of great economic value, but their numbers are no longer sustained by recruitment from the wild. Elephant round-ups rarely take place and stocks are being supplemented from calves born from already domesticated cows. Elephants are, however, difficult to breed in captivity, partly because it is almost impossible to control bulls when they are in musth and partly because cows with small calves cannot work for a long time. Calves do not begin work until 15 years old. The cows are therefore condemned to a life of celibacy and toil. Nevertheless they occasionally contrive to mate with wild bulls. On my last visit to Nepal my riding elephant suddenly gave birth to a delightful little bull calf, to the amazement of her mahout, who had been quite unaware that she was pregnant. She had evidently mated one night while turned out to feed in the forest. The traditional method of recruitment, known as the *khedda*, involved driving wild elephants into stockades, where they were chained until trained. The rounding up and driving of wild herds caused great psychological disturbance to such sensitive creatures and this method was condemned by conservationists. It is no longer used today in India, though still practised in Bangladesh and Myanmar (Burma). One of the last *kheddas* in India took place in the Nagarhole region in the 1970s. Another method used in north-east India is the so-called *mela shikar*, in which wild elephants are lassooed from trained domestic elephants. Less harm and panic in the herd would arise if selected animals were dart-gunned with tranquillizing drugs.

A scientific symposium was held in 1982 at the Jaldapara Sanctuary in West Bengal to examine the very difficult problem of the conservation and management of Asian Elephants. The problem is compounded by the obvious fact that the more wild populations are compressed by the growing destruction of their forest habitat, and the more groups become broken up and isolated, the greater the difficulty of controlling their ravages on plantations of oil-palm, sugar-cane, rice and other crops. When elephants are hungry it is extremely difficult to prevent them from doing serious damage. Crowds of villagers try to stop them by banging gongs, waving torches, throwing spears and shooting at them with crop-protection guns. The frightened elephants are then liable to charge the crowd and not only trample the crops, but sometimes also knock down village houses, killing people in the process. It was shown at the symposium that there are two practical means of preventing such losses. One is to station *koonkis* (domesticated elephants trained for the capture of wild ones) to guard the crops; wild elephants are apparently terrified by them, perhaps because of their close association with humans, although this does not prevent occasional mating with them when domesticated females are on heat. The other is to erect simple two-strand electrified fences, which the elephants soon learn to respect. Protected areas for ensuring the long-term survival of elephants need to be large, typically a few thousand square kilometres, but few of these exist. The Government of India launched Project Elephant in 1991, along the lines of Project Tiger. The aims of the project are directed towards more effective management of elephant habitats and populations, including measures to reduce straying by elephants in order to mitigate damage to crops and the loss of human life.

Riding a well-trained elephant is still incomparably the best method for seeing wildlife in India. I have often been able to approach Tigers and other big game animals to within ten or twelve metres by this means. Only a slowly paddled canoe on a river can compare with the silence of an elephant's progress through the jungle. Its instant response to a whispered command from the mahout, or to the pressure of his bare foot, is a revelation to those unaccustomed to the intelligence of these mighty animals.

The second largest animal of the subcontinent is the Great One-horned Rhinoceros. Of the world's five species, only the African White Rhinoceros exceeds it in weight. Its single stubby horn is rarely longer than 38 centimetres, the majority being much shorter. More than any other species it has a distinctly prehistoric appearance because of its massively folded hide, which is studded with rounded tubercules resembling rivet heads, recalling the riveted armour on a 1918 army tank. Formerly distributed throughout the Gangetic plain and even in the middle reaches of the Indus in Pakistan (where a pair from Nepal has been reintroduced to the Lal Suhanra National Park), it is now restricted to a very few areas, such as the Kaziranga National Park in Assam, the Jaldapara Sanctuary in West Bengal and the Royal Chitwan National Park in Nepal. The total number surviving is about 1300 in India and 400 in Nepal and they are breeding successfully under

War elephants carved from stone in a tenth century wall frieze at the Lakshmana temple, Khajuraho.

protection. In order to widen the distribution, rhinos have been reintroduced in 1984 to Dudwa National Park, Uttar Pradesh, and in 1986 to Royal Bardia National Park, Nepal. Reports indicate that 238 rhinos were poached in India between 1982 and 1985 but this rate of attrition has slowed down considerably in recent years due to successful protection programmes.

Like the African and other Asian species, the One-horned Rhinoceros has suffered persistent persecution for the supposed medicinal and to a lesser extent the aphrodisiac value of its horn. Currently, Indian rhino horn fetches the highest price in Taiwan where, in 1990, its wholesale value was $45,000 per kilogram. This escalating price is having an adverse effect on conservation: in Assam, 58 rhinos were killed in 1989, and in Nepal's Royal Chitwan National Park 12 rhinos were taken by poachers between August 1989 and July 1990. Perhaps it is the extraordinary appearance and power of a rhino that have suggested magical properties to the superstitious, for every part of its carcass is valued. Even its urine was bottled and sold in Indian zoos as a cure for asthma. But to kill a 2 1/2 ton rhino merely to cut off its horn, is like destroying a cathedral in order to steal the cross from its spire.

The much smaller Sumatran Rhinoceros, which once occupied the hills of Assam, may still wander occasionally from Myanmar (Burma) into the Hill Tracts of Bangladesh. In 1967 one was shot near Cox's Bazar and its carcass sold in small pieces in Chittagong for the equivalent of some $1200. The Javan Rhinoceros, which occurred in the Sundarbans until 1900, is nearing extinction in Java.

One-horned Rhinoceroses are more solitary than their African relations. Like all rhinos they are rather morose and of uncertain temper, not hesitating, if accompanied by a calf, to charge an intruding elephant. In a close attack they slash upwards with their powerful incisors rather than with their horns. I have watched two bull rhinos fighting and the collision was like that of two high-speed trains. They can run surprisingly quickly and I have been more frightened by them at night when camping in their neighbourhood than ever I was by Tigers, which prefer to avoid contact with humans. However, One-horned Rhinoceroses can be observed without difficulty if one's elephant is well trained, as they are, for example, in the Kaziranga or Chitwan national parks.

Among the many even-toed ungulates of the subcontinent - the wild oxen, sheep, goats, antelopes and boar - the massive Gaur, or Indian Bison, takes pride of place. Standing nearly two metres at the shoulder and weighing 900 kilograms or more, a bull Gaur is a magnificent animal. Its sleek hide is a gleaming black, with strikingly white 'stockings'. Its horns are short and curved and its enormous shoulders are ridged as far as the middle of its back. In spite of such an imposing appearance, however, Gaur are timid, forest-loving creatures, moving about in small family herds and descending from the hills to graze in the valleys at dawn and again in late afternoon. Their only enemy is the Tiger, which preys on the smaller cows and calves, very rarely tackling a full-grown bull. These splendid animals are now chiefly restricted to the eastern

In Nepal's Royal Chitwan National Park, tourists are conveyed through the jungle for game viewing on trained elephants.

and southern hill forests. They can be seen in such protected areas as the Bandipur in Karnataka State and the adjoining Mudumalai in Tamil Nadu. There are a few in the Kanha National Park in Madhya Pradesh and I have occasionally seen a herd in the western part of the Chitwan in Nepal when fresh grass was just emerging. Gaur have never been domesticated, although hybrids with domestic cattle do occur occasionally. It seems possible that such crosses led to the creation of the Gayal, or Mithun, which resembles a rather small Gaur with straighter horns. Gayal are at least now and then domesticated, not as draught animals but for purposes of religious sacrifice, by some of the forest tribes such as the Moghs and Chakmas of the Hill Tracts. However, my companion Eric Hosking and I were once chased along a river bank in the Hill Tracts by a couple of bull Gayals, which gave no evidence whatever of being domesticated. Their charge was, in fact, rather spectacular.

Almost as massively built as the Gaur, the Wild Asiatic Water Buffalo is a much more aggressive animal. Whereas domestic buffaloes are the epitome of docility and are led or ridden by tiny children in the paddyfields, their wild relatives are extremely shy of humans. They can be dangerous if approached too closely and not infrequently kill domestic bulls which show interest in their cows. Not many of them are left now and most of the survivors are restricted to the swampy grasslands and cane-brakes of Assam. The Kaziranga National Park and Manas Sanctuary are among the best places to see them. They are also found in the Bastar forests of Madhya Pradesh, and there are some 90 in Koshi Tappu Wildlife Reserve in Nepal but the entire population is reported to have hybridized with feral water buffalo. Wild Yaks are no longer known to occur south of the main Himalayan divide, but domesticated Yaks can be seen in the higher levels of Nepal and Ladakh and also Zums, which are hybrids between Yak cows and domestic Brahminy bulls.

The four types of wild sheep of the Himalayas can be seen only by those prepared to climb to the high altitudes where they live. They are all hunted by the hill tribes and, in spite of their being officially protected, may also be shot by foreign trophy hunters and embassy officials who bribe the local authorities. The most splendid of the four is the Marco Polo Sheep of the Hunza region and the Russian Pamirs, whose great outward-curving, deeply wrinkled horns are much more massive than those of the famous Big-horn Sheep of the American Rockies. The very similar Nayan, or Tibetan Sheep, of Ladakh, Nepal and Sikkim, have horns almost as large, although they never exceed a single circle, whereas those of the Marco Polo have an additional outward curve. Both are distinctive races, or subspecies, of the Argali Sheep, whose distribution stretches from the Pamirs to Outer Mongolia and throughout the Tibetan Plateau. Much smaller and more numerous in the mountains of Gilgit, Astor and Ladakh are the various races of the smaller-horned Urial, or Shapu; other races occur in the Salt Range and Kirthar Range in Pakistan, where they are more easily seen. The rather curious Bharal, or so-called Blue Sheep, which occupies the Himalayas at altitudes of 3000 to 5000 metres in northern Pakistan, Ladakh, Nepal and Sikkim, is now regarded as more closely related to the goats. Its horns are smooth and curved backwards, giving it a somewhat typically goat-like character. It is extremely difficult to approach and because its slate-blue hide merges perfectly with the colour of the rocks, is very difficult to observe until it moves.

There are five species of wild goat, all living in the mountains and all amazingly agile creatures which appear to defy the laws of gravity with impunity. I have seen some of them, such as the Ibex, running at full speed down almost vertical rocks which offered no apparent footholds. Even the rather heavily built and long-haired Markhor, which has massive corkscrew horns, leads his harem at astonishing speed when alarmed. The Wild Goat, or Sind Ibex, is very like the Ibex, but with a grey rather than a buffish coat; its long, curved horns are slightly shorter than the 1.40 metres attained by the Ibex. Both are found at the western end of the Himalayas, a smaller race of the Sind Ibex also inhabiting the southern Kirthar Range in Pakistan. Although shooting has reduced the populations of these species, the main reason for their decline has been the introduction of diseases, such as anthrax, carried by domestic goats. I have seen domestic flocks feeding at 4300 metres where Markhor and Urial were also present. The two other goat species, the Himalayan and the Nilgiri Tahrs, are very distinctive and have short, back-curved horns. The Himalayan lives among the most spectacular crags and sheer cliffs up to an altitude of 5200 metres and feeds on the alpine pastures. It has a handsome golden-brown coat of long, shaggy hair. Its relative the Nilgiri Tahr, when adult, has a blackish-brown coat with a whitish patch on its lower back and lacks the heavy mane of the Himalayan species. It is restricted to the higher altitudes (about 2000 metres) of the Western Ghats where the total population is about 2200.

The subcontinent has three species of goat-antelopes, the Goral, the Serow and the Takin. All three have goat-like characteristics such as short, cylindrical horns and short tails, and live in the mountains. The Goral also has some resemblance to a Chamois, except for its horns, which lack the latter's terminal hook. The Serow is much larger and more ungainly, with long, donkey-like ears and blackish-brown hide. Both species are widespread in the Himalayas, the Goral frequenting more open habitat in small groups, while the more solitary Serow prefers dense forest and precipitous terrain. The Takin, which lives in the Bhutan Himalayas and the Mishmi Hills, is even more ungainly, with a heavy-lipped, cow-like face and dense, shaggy fur which brings to

mind a Yak. Its thick neck and short curved horns, on the other hand, recall those of a Wildebeest, yet it has no obvious relatives except the North American Musk Ox, and is an altogether curious creature. Visitors to Bhutan can see Takin in the small reserve at Thimphu, the capital city.

The great herds of gazelles and deer which once roamed the subcontinent have long since disappeared, although they could be seen in fair numbers until the 1940s. The dainty little Chinkara Gazelle is the most agile of the group and, although exterminated in most of its former range, still survives in the Indian deserts and the open plains of the Deccan, as well as in the foothills of the Salt Range and in some other semi-desert areas of Pakistan. The little-known Tibetan Gazelle and the long-horned Tibetan Antelope or Chiru occur in the northern parts of Ladakh. The handsome Blackbuck, an antelope, was the favourite target of hunters from the days of the Moghuls onwards and was very nearly exterminated. Fortunately, many Maharajahs kept captive herds in order to enjoy the sport of seeing them chased and killed by captive Cheetahs or packs of dogs and some of these herds survived. There is a special Blackbuck sanctuary in the Velavadar National Park in Gujarat and at Talchappar in Rajasthan. In Pakistan they had almost totally disappeared by the 1960s, but with the initial aid of the Word Wide Fund for Nature some were reintroduced into the Lal Suhanra National Park in Cholistan from Texas, where huge herds originally introduced from Pakistan are now thriving in thousands on some of the big ranches. Others have since been reintroduced to Pakistan from India. Such co-operation in spite of political differences is very gratifying to conservationists. Both Chinkara and Blackbuck are protected by the Bishnoi community in western Rajasthan and many thousands wander freely through crops and eat their fill.

The Four-horned Antelope, or Chowsingha, is a solitary little animal which inhabits the tall-grass hilly regions of peninsula India. It is the only species with two pairs of short, spiky horns, which are carried by the male only. Standing barely 60 centimetres high, it is difficult to observe, but its shrill, whistling call can frequently be heard.

Few animals are more ungainly than the Nilgai, whose name means 'blue cow'. Everything about it looks wrong. Its horns look uselessly small (though surprisingly, one killed a man in Bhopal); it is too high at the shoulder and too sloping at the haunches; when it gallops, it does so in an ungainly giraffe-like manner and holds its head unnaturally high. Yet it is a successful animal, perhaps chiefly because its cow-like appearance prompts Hindus to give it religious protection and Moslem hunters to disdain shooting such a worthless creature.

Of the eight deer species, the most familiar is the Chital, or Spotted Deer, which, with its closely spotted rufous coat, is often regarded as the most beautiful of the world's many deer. For this reason it is a favourite in parks and zoos. In the wild it can be seen in most of the forests below the Indian and Nepalese Himalayas.

The four largest deer are the Sambar, the Barasingha, the Thamin and the Hangul. The last-mentioned, which is also called the Kashmir Stag, closely resembles the European Red Deer. These handsome animals are restricted to the moist temperate forests in the northern part of Kashmir. They are most easily seen in the Dachigam National Park, a few miles north of Srinagar, and perhaps in the Gamgul Siahbehi Sanctuary in Himachal Pradesh. The Sambar, India's largest deer, is numerous and occurs over a wide altitudinal range. The heavily maned stags carry long, powerful antlers which divide into two forks, with long, curved brow-times.

The Barasingha, or Swamp Deer, is paler in colour than the Sambar. Its antlers are readily distinguishable because they branch into numerous, up-turned points and the brow-tines are more curved. There are three distinct races that are now recognized: *Cervus d. duvauceli*, which has slightly splayed hooves and lives in swampy areas of Dudwa and the Nepalese *terai*; *C. d. ranjitsinhi* in similar habitat in Assam, and *C. d. branderi* with smaller, closer hooves appropriate to the hard, open ground where it lives in Madhya Pradesh. The largest concentrations of the duvauceli race are along the Nepalese frontier. A fine herd can be seen in the Dudwa National Park, created by my old friend Billy Arjan Singh, but numbers have declined considerably from 1400 in 1981 to 800 in 1988/89. There is another large population of 900 in the Royal Sukla Phanta Wildlife Reserve in western Nepal, which I helped to create in 1972. The Kaziranga National Park in Assam is the main region of the *ranjitsinhi* race. The *branderi* race is easily seen in the Kanha National Park in Madhya Pradesh, which in my opinion is the best in India.

In the low scrub-jungle of south-east Asia lives the Thamin, or Brow-antlered Deer. Its range extends westward only as far as the Manipur region of India, where the Manipur race, locally known as the Sangai, can still be seen in the *phumdi*, the floating swamp of Keibul Lamjao National Park. It resembles the Barasingha except for its distinctively curved antlers, forming a forward-pointing semi-circle from the brow-tine to the tip, which has only three or four rather blunt points.

There are three much smaller deer species: the Muntjak, the Hog Deer and the Musk Deer. The first two are quite numerous. Muntjak, or Barking Deer, stand 75 centimetres at the shoulder and have stubby little 7 centimetre antlers with two prongs, which rise from distinctive pedicles near the eyes. They live in thickly wooded hills along the Himalayas and in the central and southern Indian forests. Though shy, their dog-like barking call is easily imitated and I once called one out to the edge of a forest track by this means.

The origin of the Hog Deer's name is obvious: its rotund shape and pig-like movements as it scuttles through the undergrowth, with its head held very low. Although related to the well-antlered Chital, the Hog Deer male has very small two-pointed antlers like the Muntjak, but also two little brow-tines. Its habitat is dense grass along river-banks and in the plains, where it suffers heavy predation by Leopards and other large cats. Even Tigers do not disdain such tasty little creatures, pouncing on them in the long grass as a domestic cat will on a field mouse.

Musk Deer occur up to 4400 metres in the Himalayas, living mainly in the high birch-rhododendron forests from Kashmir through Nepal and Bhutan to Arunachal Pradesh. Other species live in Siberia and China, where they are farmed. They are distinctive little animals, with very round bodies, elongated heads and large ears, but no antlers. The so-called musk-pod, a sexual gland lying beneath the abdominal skin of the male, has been their downfall, being highly prized as a base for the manufacture of perfumes and for various medicinal purposes throughout Asia.

The elusive little Chevrotain, or Mouse Deer, a delightful Walt Disneyesque animal not much larger than a rabbit, is related to the deer family but more primitive in many of its features. It has delicate, pencil-thin legs, with four toes to each foot and a striped and spotted body. Like the Musk Deer, it lacks antlers and has projecting canine teeth. It is difficult to believe that these miniature creatures, flitting like small shadows through the litter on a forest floor, survive the constant predation of the many carnivores, birds of prey, Eagle Owls and Pythons which share the forest with them.

Only one species of the horse family is found in the subcontinent – the Wild Ass. There are two races, the Indian, which is now restricted to Gujarat, and the Tibetan, which occurs in the Ladakh area of Jammu and Kashmir, in northern Sikkim and also in the extreme north of Pakistan. Herds of the Indian race used to roam in thousands across the desert regions of India and Baluchistan, but today it can be found only in the saline clay desert of the Little Rann of Kutch, which it shares with Chinkara Gazelles and Nilgai. A few occasionally wander into the Great Rann on the frontier between Gujarat and the Thar Desert in Pakistan. Living in a frontier region, they have been much persecuted by soldiers, who enjoy chasing them in jeeps. In Pakistan the soldiers assured me they never shot Wild Asses, but that local poachers did so in order to make suitcases out of their tanned hides. An adjacent military firing range is another hazard. It seems likely, however, that the decline in the population of Asses is mainly the result of competition for the very limited grazing by domestic cattle and of diseases such as African horse fever which the latter have introduced. Their population dropped to a record low of 362 in 1967, but by 1983 had recovered to almost 2000. The Little Rann has been declared a Sanctuary, but the future for the Indian Wild Ass remains a cause for concern. Other races of the species still survive in Tibet, Mongolia and Iran. The Syrian race is now extinct.

The dog family is well represented. Wolves have become scarce in India, where only 1000 to 2000 may remain; but they can still be seen in the barren highlands of Ladakh and in the dry regions of India and Pakistan, where they take a toll of domestic cattle, goats and sheep. In Ladakh, Wolves are traditionally trapped in deep stone pits baited with a tethered donkey, but more often they are poisoned, or shot while attacking domestic flocks. Those living on the Tibetan plateau are almost black and have much longer fur than the lowland Wolves of Pakistan and peninsular India. Occasionally, when hungry, they take to killing children around villages, although nowadays reports of such behaviour are extremely rare. Jackals are fairly common everywhere and, like the rarer Striped Hyena, are useful scavengers; the latter are nevertheless much disliked for their habit of disinterring human corpses. The weird and ghostly crying of Jackals at night used to be one of the typical sounds of India. In chorus it has a nightmare quality though less frequently heard today. Foxes, too, are numerous and there are three distinctive races of the Eurasian Red Fox – the Hill Fox, the Desert Fox and the White-footed Fox. Another species, the Indian Fox, occurs throughout India.

Probably the most interesting canine is the Dhole, or Wild Dog. Like its African counterpart it is gregarious, hunting in packs, all members of the group helping to feed the young. Larger than the Jackal, it has a rufous colour and inhabits both open and forested regions from the Himalayas to the southern peninsula. It hunts in daylight, the pack pursuing its quarry at a relentless, loping gait, accelerating with a chorus of excited yapping in the final climax when the victim is surrounded and brought down. I find this sound particularly thrilling and full of menace. The communal skill of a hunting pack is impressive. A herd of deer is first stampeded, then a sickly animal or a fawn is cut out and separated from the herd and the chase begins. The victim very seldom escapes. If deer are scarce, Dhole packs do not hesitate to take on such formidable animals as Gaur, Buffalo, young Rhinoceroses or even Tigers, although many members of the pack may be killed in such encounters.

Monkeys are part of almost every Indian scene, crowding around villages and boldly entering cities, where they help themselves to food at wayside stalls and mingle with the traffic. They are rarely molested, although a few species such as the Golden Leaf Monkey of the Sankosh River region on the Bhutan frontier have been known to be killed for their beautiful fur.

The common monkey in northern India is the Rhesus Macaque, which is distinguished from all other species by its red bottom. It can be seen around every town, temple and railway station, begging for food. There are six related and more localized species – the slightly larger Assamese Macaque, which does not have the characteristic red bottom, the Stump-tailed Macaque of the eastern Himalayan foothills, the Pig-tailed Macaque of the Naga Hills, with an upstanding arched tail, the long-tailed Bonnet Macaque of the southern peninsula, the crab-eating macaque of the Nicobar Islands, and the handsome but scarce Lion-tailed Macaque of the Malabar rain forests in the Ashambu Hills of the Western Ghats, the Anamalai Sanctuary in Tamil Nadu and the Nellcampathi Hills in Kerala. The Lion-tailed, with its luxuriant mane of whitish hair and a tufted tail, is now listed as an endangered species threatened by the destruction of its habitat. In 1996, there were an estimated 4500.

The second most plentiful monkey is the Common Langur, also known as the Hanuman Monkey. Shrines to the monkey-god Hanuman are numerous, particularly in Nepal. All the Langur species are extremely agile, long-limbed and long-tailed; their tails are not, however, prehensile like those of the South American monkeys. Common Langurs inhabit most Indian forests and I have seen them both at sea level and at 3500 metres in the Himalayas, where they have a particular fondness for eating rhododendron flowers. It is a delight to watch them leaping from tree to tree along the highways, or posed in graceful groups on the steps of ancient temples. They are invaluable companions in the jungle, giving immediate warning of the presence of Tigers or Leopards, which they follow with excited chattering from the safety of the tree-tops. The beautiful Golden Leaf Monkey has already been mentioned. In addition there is the Capped Langur of Assam and the Chittagong Hill Tracts and the Nilgiri Langur, or Nilgiri Leaf Monkey, of the Western Ghats. Occasionally the closely related Phayre's Leaf Monkey occurs in Tripura and Bangladesh. My expedition of 1967 discovered and filmed in Sylhet a previously unrecorded species which proved to be a small colony of Dusky Leaf Monkeys; these were evidently vagrants from Myanmar (Burma).

Two very small but fascinating little primates also inhabit the region – the Slow Loris and the Slender Loris. Although strictly nocturnal and very secretive, and therefore unlikely to be seen, they are often kept as pets in forest villages, where visitors may come across them. They belong to the Lemur family and have enormous, owl-like eyes and very round, pale, furry bodies. Feeding at night in the trees, they move in ultra-slow motion until they come upon an insect, which is then grabbed with both hands. Their grip is vice-like and quite difficult to release. The Slow Loris is the larger of the two, with a length of about 30 centimetres. The Slender Loris is barely 23 centimetres long and has prominent ears and grotesquely spindly little legs. It is a rather pathetic sight to see these inoffensive small creatures with such big-eyed, infantile expressions, tied to a post in full sunlight, for they need the darkness of the forest and will not survive long on village tit-bits.

Villagers in India also frequently keep captive civets and mongooses, both of which are easily tamed. There are half a dozen civet species, the most common being the Large and the Small Indian Civets, which are readily recognized by their boldly banded tails. All have long, sinuous bodies and long tails, with rather short legs and pointed muzzles. The Small Civet is seen everywhere except in high forest, whereas the Large is chiefly restricted to the Himalayan region. Both are omnivorous, with an unfortunate liking for raiding chicken coops and orchards. Another widespread species is the Palm Civet, or Toddy Cat, which is also frequently domesticated and can be seen scavenging in towns as well as villages. Unlike the two previously mentioned, it has a plain, unbanded tail. All the civets are useful as voracious and skilled hunters of rats.

For sheer agility and non-stop activity, no animals surpass the mongooses, of which there are five species in India and Pakistan. The one most widely seen both in the wild and as a domestic pet is the common Grey Mongoose. Many Europeans have learned to their cost that while mongooses make enchanting and affectionate pets, the speed with which they can totally wreck the curtains, cushions and ornaments in a home has to be seen to be believed. These world-famous little animals, immortalized by Rudyard Kipling's Rikitikitavi, invariably draw crowds when exhibited by snake-charmers in contests with cobras. The fact that the snakes have usually had their poison-glands drained or removed makes little difference, because the mongoose's erected bristling fur and lightning reactions protect it. Nevertheless, in the wild, mongooses, though remarkably resistant to snake poison, do occasionally succumb to the bite of a Cobra or a Krait. Villagers keep them as

pets not only to combat snakes, but to control rats, mice and scorpions, which are obviously relished.

The Small Indian Mongoose, which is only half the size of the Grey, is also widespread and hunts in daylight. A distinctive race called the Desert Mongoose has a pale sandy colour, but is almost rufous in the Sind desert, where family parties hunt mice and gerbils. There are three larger, much less common species, the Stripe-necked of the Western Ghats, the Brown of southern India and the interesting Crab-eating Mongoose of Nepal and Assam. The last-mentioned species is the only aquatic member of the family, swimming and diving like an otter and feeding on fish, crabs and frogs.

In the Himalayan and southern parts of India, local races of the European Otter are found, while the very similar Smooth Otter occupies the whole region except for desert areas. One of its strongholds is the Sundarbans, where it is trained to drive fish into nets. Nets are lowered between two boats and the otters skilfully circle and drive the fish into them. Afterwards they climb on board, where each is given a fish, which is munched with little chirruping cries of obvious satisfaction. The otters are then permitted a siesta and a grooming session before renewing their work. The Bengali fishermen seem fond of their willing helpers and treat them well. The smaller, so-called Clawless Otter (which nevertheless has rudimentary claws) is very locally distributed only in some hill regions, the plains of Assam and lower Bengal.

Apart from the three otters, the fauna of the subcontinent is enriched by nearly two dozen other species of the family Mustelidae – the various martens, weasels, polecats, ferret-badgers, badgers and ratels. Then there are the Insectivores – the various shrews, hedgehogs and moles. And the very numerous families of bats and rodents, squirrels and flying squirrels, the porcupines and the hares, the pigs and the pangolins.

A familiar animal of the temperate Himalayan and Assamese forests is the handsome Yellow-throated Marten, which occurs at altitudes up to 4000 metres. It is an agile hunter high in the trees or on the ground, occasionally killing animals as large as young Musk Deer, but usually preying on squirrels and birds, including pheasants and Snow Partridges. It has a fondness for fruit and the nectar of the Silk Cotton tree flowers, which it helps to pollinate. Its distinctive southern relative, the Nilgiri Marten, has more uniformly dark brown upper-parts and reddish forequarters. On the upper forest edges the Indian race of the European Stone Marten is fairly common as far east as Sikkim. Between 2400 and 4500 metres is the habitat of the Long-tailed Marmot and above them live the shorter-tailed Himalayan Marmots. Both are colonial-breeding and are familiar to all trekkers at these heights, sitting at the entrances of their burrows. I find their shrill whistling alarm cries rather welcome and reassuring in the oppressive silence of the high barrens.

Choosing from a long list of Indian bats, the great Indian Flying Fox can scarcely be missed as it is so conspicuous in many towns in India, Pakistan and Bangladesh. Its electrocuted corpses hang from countless power lines, looking like broken umbrellas. At dusk great flocks sally forth to feed on mangoes, figs and bananas. By day the flocks hang upside-down like giant fruits from the trees in city parks, cackling noisily and fanning themselves with their black wings. They are handsome creatures, with bright rufous fur and dog-like heads. In flight their wings have a spread of more than one metre and are flapped slowly, giving a crow-like rather than a bat-like impression. Like their smaller relatives the Fruit Bats, they are useful as pollinators of the fruit-bearing jungle trees, carrying pollen on their heads from tree to tree when feeding or drinking nectar from the flowers. The very striking Painted Bat has brilliant orange, vermilion and black patterned wings, and has been described as the most colourful mammal in the world. It is, however, a solitary species and seen only with good fortune.

A considerable number of very beautifully coloured squirrels and flying squirrels inhabit the forests. A few, such as the Kashmir Woolly Flying Squirrel, live at high altitudes in the Himalayas and have very copious fur to withstand the cold. Although some are as large as rabbits, they glide from tree to tree for quite astonishing distances on the extended membranes between their wrists and ankles, looking like flying tea-trays. Among the small squirrels, the species which every visitor to the subcontinent will see is the little

The Lion-tailed Macaque is an endemic species from the shola forests of the Western Ghats in south-western India. Today it is under severe threat of extinction due to habitat destruction.

Palm Squirrel, which in northern India and Pakistan usually has five stripes along its back and in the south three. It must be one of the most numerous and widespread of all the local animals. With its striped back and self-confident behaviour it is invariably likened by visiting Americans to the rather similar American Chipmunk.

Driving at night in forested regions, motorists often see Indian Porcupines crossing the road; the great mounds of earth which they excavate at the entrance to their burrows are conspicuous in many areas. These powerful animals, which can weigh as much as 18 kilograms, do a lot of damage to rootcrops and also de-bark fruit trees. They can be kept in captivity only in concrete enclosures, or they will dig their way to freedom in a matter of minutes.. In the wild they are almost invulnerable to predation because of their long, bristling quills. Leopards appear to be the only predators which occasionally succeed in killing them, which they do by going for the unprotected head. Tigers, which are less agile, cannot resist trying to kill them, but invariably the Porcupine backs swiftly into its pursuer, driving its quills into the Tiger's face and chest. Dead Tigers have been found with festering quills embedded even in their lungs.

Another conspicuous animal, which is occasionally seen tethered to a post in a village, is the armour-plated Indian Pangolin. Also called the Scaly Anteater, its body and tail are protected by strong, overlapping scales. When frightened, it instantly curls up into a tight ball. I once tried to pry open this

The rare and elusive Pygmy Hog of northern Assam, among the most endangered of the world's mammals.

defence but found the muscular contraction impregnable. The Pangolin is an inoffensive animal, which feeds on termites and ants and has a dignified, ambling gait, walking with the long, curved claws of its fore-feet turned inwards to support its weight. It is still fairly plentiful in the lowland areas and is replaced in Nepal and the northeastern states by the smaller Chinese Pangolin.

Wild Boar represent a considerable economic problem because of their devastation of crops. In areas where the Tigers and Leopards which control their numbers have been exterminated, the farmers are suffering heavy losses and now recognize the value of these predators. A full-grown male is a formidable animal. It can weigh more than 200 kilograms and is capable of killing even a Tiger with its powerful 20-centimetre tusks. A tiny and defenceless relative, the Pygmy Hog, was believed to be extinct by 1958, but was rediscovered in 1971 on the Paneery tea estate in Assam. I had the pleasure of handling a female in captivity. It measured only 26 centimetres at the shoulder, had no tusks and only three pairs of teats instead of the six of the Wild Boar. A small population of these delightful little animals is protected within the Manas Sanctuary, but despite careful management the population of perhaps 500 is thought to have declined. [Meanwhile, a successful breeding programme in Guwahati holds out hope of safeguarding this species and reintroducing it to suitable habitat in north Assam].

Finally, two interesting and related aquatic mammals deserve mention, the Gangetic and Indus Dolphins. Five species of dolphins and the Little Indian Porpoise can be seen in the estuaries or off-shore waters of the subcontinent. The Gangetic and Indus Dolphins have been the subject of long research and are now listed as threatened species. Unlike most of their kind they are not gregarious. They have only rudimentary eyes and feed on crustaceans on river-beds, rarely if ever entering salt water,

although descending into semi-saline estuaries where they are frequently caught in fishnets. They occur far inland in the Ganges, Brahmaputra and Indus. I have seen Gangetic Dolphins as far inland as the Rapti River in Nepal. A study has been made of the survival problems of the Indus species and the government has established a game reserve for them between the Sukkur and Guddu barrages, where they increased in number under protection from an estimated 150 in 1974 to over 400 by 1986.

A Paradise for Birds

The Indian subcontinent is a positive paradise for both amateur bird-watchers and serious ornithologists. If Sri Lanka is included, it has over 1200 species and distinctive subspecies of birds, a figure surpassed only in South America. Europe has a mere 630 or so, including vagrants. As my friend Peter Jackson has shown, it is possible to see 150 different species in a single day on a car journey around the Delhi area including Sultanpur, where a sanctuary has been established. On my various explorations I have managed to see only about 800, or considerably less than half of the total species. The reason for this is that many of them are restricted to very small and remote areas. The great diversity of species is, of course, again a reflection of the many different climatic and vegetational zones available for their development.

Although the majority of birds are of tropical Oriental origin, an almost equal number originated either in the African or the Palaearctic (that is to say European or north Asian) regions. About 300 species, chiefly ducks, cranes, shore-birds, swallows and flycatchers, are migrants which enter India from central Asia at each end of the Himalayas, either down the Indus valley, or from north-eastern Asia by way of the Brahmaputra. Some of the birds pass directly over the Himalayas. Bar-headed Geese, for example, have been seen over the peak of Everest itself, in other words flying at an altitude of about nine kilometres above sea level! The Rajah of Punial gave me an identification ring taken from the leg of a migrant Bar-headed Goose which he had shot crossing the high peaks of Hunza; later investigation showed that it had been ringed in north-central USSR. Many other species are merely altitudinal migrants, passing regularly back and forth from the high mountain slopes where they breed only as far as the valleys to winter. But a few, such as the hardy Snow Partridge and Snow Pigeon, contrive to nest successfully at an altitude of 5000 metres. For ornithologists interested in mass migration there are two much favoured Himalayan areas. One is the Kali Gandaki gorge, between the 8000 metre peaks of Annapurna and Dhaulagiri; the other is the high valleys of Ladakh, which are more difficult of access for the average visitor.

Birds are seldom molested in India. There was however a thriving export trade of about 2 million wild-caught birds every year, chiefly the small, colourful finches, parakeets and mynahs, for the foreign cage-bird market. An extremely high mortality was involved, 50 per cent or more of the birds being dead on arrival. A total of 300 species were involved in this nefarious trade which, following stricter control measures, now accounts for some 100,000 birds.

Among the most extravagantly colourful birds are the numerous parakeets, woodpeckers and kingfishers, which are easily observed. Noisy flocks of the emerald-green Rose-ringed and Large Parakeets are common in many cities, the former nesting confidently beneath roof-tiles or in holes in wayside trees. Unfortunately, though so beautiful, their flocks do serious damage to grain crops. I have seen as many as 250 on a single field of millet. They are successful and invasive birds. Their smaller relative the Plum-headed Parakeet occupies the forested areas from Nepal southward and the Murree Hills in Pakistan. In the moist deciduous forests of the lower Himalayan region one finds the Red-breasted Parakeet and at higher altitudes, the whole length of the mountain range, the Slatey-headed Parakeet. The short-tailed green and crimson Lorikeet is more restricted to the eastern hills, Bangladesh and the Bombay region.

There are no fewer than 28 different kingfishers. They vary in size from the big Stork-billed, which is as large as a Jackdaw, to the tiny, jewel-like Three-toed, little bigger than a European Wren. Nearly all are brilliantly coloured. Some, such as the Black and

White Pied and Lesser Pied, frequent almost every stream, pond and water-tank, others are found only in tidal and coastal regions. Some are fish-eaters, others occur far inland in dry areas and feed on locusts, lizards, mice and small birds. In particularly rich feeding areas, such as the mangrove swamps of the Sundarbans, many kingfisher species occupy the same habitat, though selecting different food and therefore without competing.

The russet-coated Rufous Woodpecker favours open secondary jungle and tea plantations; it has the intriguing habit of nesting in the globular communal nests of ferocious tree-ants without evicting them. The ants merely seal off their passage-ways to the bird's nest cavity. A South American woodpecker, the Campo Flicker, has a rather similar habit of nesting in occupied termite mounds. Two other very colourful and numerous families are the sunbirds and the bee-eaters. Many Western visitors to India take the sunbirds to be hummingbirds because of their darting flight, iridescent plumage and habit of taking nectar from flowers. Hummingbirds, however, are restricted to the Americas. The 25 species and subspecies of Indian sunbirds not only have longer legs, but also normal wings instead of the stiff, narrow wings of the typical hummingbird. Their more soberly coloured relatives, the Spider-hunters, are distinguished by their very long, decurved bills. The six different bee-eaters have a graceful swallow-like flight and colourful plumage, although none quite compares with the spectacular Carmine Bee-eater of Africa. Another brilliantly coloured bird which few visitors to India or Pakistan are likely to miss seeing perched on wayside telephone posts is the Indian Roller. In flight it displays a striking combination of shining light blue, dark blue and orange. About the size of a Jay, it gets its name from its aerobatic tumbling display-flight.

Although the subcontinent lacks the great variety of truly melodious song-birds found in Europe and North America, it has several which compare very favourably. Probably the best of these is the Shama, a beautiful but rather shy blue-black and chestnut bird with a long tail. To my mind its song equals that of a Nightingale for purity and of an American Mockingbird for variety. Not surprisingly, some Indian girls are named Shama. Its cousin the black and white Magpie-Robin can be seen in every garden.

The hornbills are another spectacular family of birds which inhabit the mature forests of India, Nepal, Bhutan and Bangladesh. All have grotesquely large bills and share the habit of walling-up their females in their nest-holes until the young are nearly fledged. This strange practice provides maximum security against predators and particularly snakes. The sitting bird easily defends the small aperture through which she and the nestlings are fed by the male. There are five species, the largest being the Great Indian Hornbill, which is more than a metre in length, with boldly marked black and white wings and tail. In flight, its very broad wings make a distinctive singing note, like that made by those of a Mute Swan. This fine bird used to be quite numerous in the high forests of the Western Ghats, Assam and the Chittagong Hill Tracts; but all the hornbills are now suffering from the loss of the big trees on which they depend for nest-holes and also from the fact that their flesh and fat are believed by many forest tribes to have medicinal value. During the Myanmar (Burma) campaign, when fresh meat was very scarce, I once ate a hornbill which had been shot by a Naga tribesman with a bow and arrow. I recall it tasted somewhat rank, doubtless because hornbills eat lizards and snakes, as well as fruit.

Hindus regard Peafowl as sacred. Semi-tame flocks can be seen in many city parks and reserves, where they are decorative rather than interesting. I prefer to see them wild and in their full magnificence, when at dawn they come flying down the steep forested slopes of the Himalayan foothills, with the great trains of the males trailing behind them. The colourful Junglefowl, ancestors of all our domestic chickens, are also best seen and heard at dawn, when the cocks challenge the rising sun with a ringing 'cock-adoodle-doo'.

Birds of prey are relatively little persecuted and can be seen everywhere. Black Kites scavenge for refuse in every town and village and nest on roofs and window-sills. The handsome chestnut and white Brahminy Kites are almost equally numerous over sea-ports and fishing villages. Four species of vulture, the White-backed, the Long-billed, the crimson-headed King and the much smaller, yellow-faced Egyptian, squabble over the numerous

carcasses of dead animals and also over the 'towers of silence' where Parsees leave their dead to be devoured. [However, in the past decade the populations of the Long-billed and White-backed species have crashed dramatically due to the use of the veterinary drug, diclofenac, on cattle. This has a highly toxic effect on *Gyps* vultures that eat affected carrion] The long-winged Lammergeyer, or Bearded Vulture, like the Himalayan Griffon Vulture, is chiefly restricted to the Himalayas. There are about 20 species of large and small eagles, of which the rather lethargic Tawny is the most common, also half a dozen falcons and a similar number of hawks and harriers. In Pakistan, the Peregrine and its close relatives the Saker and Lagger Falcons are in constant demand by Arab falconers, who pay very high prices for them. In Sind and Punjab they are caught by desert tribesmen during their migration. A man hides in a pit over which a trellis of branches is placed. A pigeon or a dove is tethered to the branches and made to flutter until it catches the eye of a passing falcon. When the falcon stoops on the decoy, the man in the pit seizes it by the legs. Many of these birds reach Europe and the Middle East illegally and are eagerly bought for large sums of money, in spite of the heavy fines now imposed in some countries for possessing wild-caught falcons.

The bustard family, like the falcons, also suffers serious persecution and again it is the oil-rich Arabs from the Middle East who are the principal culprits. The species chiefly concerned is the Houbara Bustard. These handsome, turkey-like birds migrate each winter from the Aral Sea region in the USSR where they breed, to the deserts of Pakistan, Baluchistan and India, where they feed on the plentiful locusts. Every year hundreds of sheikhs and their numerous retinues arrive in Pakistan with fleets of Land-Rovers fitted with balloon sand-tyres in order to fly their falcons at Houbaras. Some years they have killed as many as 3000. No scarce birds can withstand such a slaughter, and Russian conservationists have complained of a 75 per cent decline in the breeding population since the hunting in Pakistan began. Having exterminated the Houbara in their own countries, the Arabs have now agreed to support a research and breeding project and the Pakistan government, in spite of benefiting financially from the annual invasion of rich falconers, has introduced restrictions on the number of birds which may be taken. A total ban on the hunting of this species would be well merited.

The larger and much more rare Great Indian Bustards live in even more parlous a situation. Standing one metre high and with long legs, they resemble miniature ostriches. Unfortunately they also represent to hungry people nearly 5 kilograms of meat and their population has been reduced to a dangerously low level of only 1400. Although they are now supposed to be strictly protected, poachers from the towns have little difficulty in killing them. They are easily seen when the males are displaying. Special reserves have now been created for these really splendid birds in the Desert Sanctuary in Rajasthan and at Karera in Madhya Pradesh. Even more scarce are their small relatives, the Bengal and Lesser Floricans, both of which are nearing extinction. The former is now restricted to the grasslands of the Nepalese terai and Assam; the latter's range extends from the Makran Coast in Pakistan through Punjab and Rajasthan south to Karnataka and Tamil Nadu. It also occurs in western Madhya Pradesh, where I count myself lucky to have seen one.

In order to see wetlands birds, there is no better or more readily accessible locality than the magnificent refuge at Bharatpur in Rajasthan, now established as the Keoladeo National Park. Once the property of the local Maharajah, it earned fame for the enormous bags of ducks which were shot there. During two visits by British Viceroys the totals exceeded 4000 in a single day. Bharatpur is now justifiably world famous, offering an unrivalled spectacle of hundreds of thousands of ducks, herons, cranes, pelicans, storks, ibises, jacanas and other aquatic birds. No fewer than 369 species of birds have been identified in the park. They can be seen very easily, simply by walking along the bunds between the many ponds. Between July and October the trees and reed-beds are crowded with nesting birds. The adjacent fields are alive with various plovers, peafowl, Sarus Cranes and a few deer. Some excellent ornithological research is being done there by the Bombay Natural History Society. Bharatpur is the only place in India where the ultra-rare Siberian Cranes come every winter, although their numbers have declined steadily in recent years from 41 in the 1984/85 winter to 3 in 1995/96 [the population has since dwindled to zero, and no Siberian Cranes have been seen at Bharatpur since 2002]. Crane hunting along the migration route is considered to be a major cause of mortality, exacerbated by drought and water management problems at Bharatpur. There the wetlands have been overrun by vegetation, following the removal of domestic water buffalo from the park, and disturbance from thousands of tourists is excessively high.[Despite its importance, the future of Bharatpur and its wildlife is gravely threatened by competition for water with local farmers, who command more votes and political sway than conservation does.]

Eight of the world's most magnificent pheasant species occupy the Himalayan region. Of these, the iridescent purple Impeyan and the Western Tragopan are the most spectacular. All, unfortunately, are hunted by the hill tribes and most are now increasingly difficult to find. The Pheasant Trust and the World Pheasant Association have been active in restoring populations by supplying eggs or young birds raised in Europe, and both India and Pakistan now have captive-breeding projects for some of the rarer species.

The desert regions of the subcontinent are no less rewarding to ornithologists. Birds of prey of many kinds are numerous and can be seen feeding on the multitude of small rodents and lizards and on the plentiful carrion of domestic animals. There are always several species of sandgrouse around the water-holes and everywhere there are interesting larks, shrikes and wheatears. The occasional jheels (lakes) in the Pakistan desert regions are invariably crowded with wading birds of many species and often with rarities such as Flamingoes or the curious little stiff-tailed White-headed Ducks. The best place to see large numbers of Flamingoes, however, is at their huge breeding colonies on the salt lakes in the Great Rann of Kutch, although the journey to get there by camel or jeep over the sun-scorched flats is pretty arduous. Temperatures can exceed 45°C, and photography is impeded by the levitations of the mirage.

To the serious ornithologist nothing can be more frustrating than the task of trying to identify the confusing host of small warblers, the 'little brown jobs' as they are often disparagingly called, and the even more numerous babblers and laughing-

Stone plaques at Bharatpur record wildfowl shoots of former days.

thrushes, of which there are no fewer than 162 species inhabiting the subcontinent. India's most famous ornithologist and conservationist, my old friend the late Dr S·lim Ali, has shown that it requires ten volumes to describe and illustrate all the birds of the region. This book, therefore, can do no more than whet the appetite of the visitor.

The Cold-blooded Creatures

No attempt to describe the wildlife of the Indian subcontinent can ignore its crocodilians, snakes and other reptiles. Of the first

mentioned there are three species – the blunt-nosed Mugger, or Marsh Crocodile, the thin-snouted, fish-eating Gharial and the larger sea-going Estuarine Crocodile. All used to be very numerous before the skin-traders got to work on them. Today they are far from plentiful and the Gharial has only just escaped extermination. Loss of habit has contributed to this decline, and the buried eggs of all the crocodilians are subject to heavy predation by monitor lizards, mongooses and many other animals. During the second World War, I remember seeing Muggers by the dozen basking on the banks of many rivers in India and Pakistan. Now such a sight is rare, but there is still a reasonable population in a few protected areas. The Gharial survived only because of strenuous efforts by the Indian and Nepalese governments following a WWF-sponsored survey, which showed that this inoffensive crocodile was on the brink of extinction. Although sometimes attaining a length of seven metres, it never attacks humans. A breeding project on the Rapti River in the Royal Chitwan National Park in Nepal was financed by the Frankfurt Zoo. By 1980, 16 crocodile rearing centres and 11 sanctuaries specifically for crocodiles had been established in the subcontinent. Many hundreds of young Gharials and Muggers have been raised from eggs taken in the wild and when they have attained a length of about 1Ω metres have been released in the local rivers. Some have been fitted with collars bearing miniature radio transmitters, so that their movements and survival can be monitored. The big salt-water Estuarine Crocodile can occasionally be seen in the tidal creeks of the Ganges, Brahmaputra and Mahanadi rivers and in some Indian coastal waters. A sanctuary has been established for them at Bhitar Kanika in Orissa, while others have been reared successfully by the Madras Crocodile Bank.

There are said to be no fewer than 236 species or distinctive subspecies of snakes in the subcontinent. Many of these can be seen in comfort in the Madras Snake Park, which was created by Romulus Whitaker with the help of the WWF as an educational project. Nearly all are not only harmless but actually beneficial to man in controlling the vast rodent population. Without snakes, mongooses and owls, India might be unable to feed itself. Even now, according to an FAO report, rats consume a tonnage of stored grain every year equivalent to the total tonnage imported into India and Bangladesh under the various Foreign Aid and Famine Relief programmes. The export of snake skins was a lucrative business until 1968, when the total reached ten million. This very harmful trade has now been banned.

There are only two really big snakes, the common Rock Python and the rather rare Reticulated Python, both of which can reach a length exceeding seven metres and a weight of 115 kilograms. They are, of course, non-poisonous and kill their prey by crushing it in their powerful coils. Small mammals are their usual prey. I know of only one human, a small boy, being a victim; but pythons often seek shelter in the thatched roofs of village houses, where their discovery can cause much excitement. I did not realize just how powerful these beautifully marked snakes are until I was involved in catching one barely five metres long for examination in the Hill Tracts. It required four strong men to hold it relatively still before we released it into the jungle.

The venomous snakes are relatively few and some are strictly regional. These are the Common, Banded and Black Kraits, the Cobras (which occur in three forms - the Monocled, the Spectacled and the Black), the King Cobra, or Hamadryad, of the rain forests, (which can occasionally attain five metres in length), the Russell's and Saw-scaled Vipers, the Coral Snakes, the Bamboo and the Himalayan Pit Vipers and the various Sea Snakes, of which the Banded is the most common. None will deliberately attack humans unless provoked or accidentally stepped upon. Nevertheless, because 75 per cent of India's people live in villages where snakes are attracted to seek vermin or shelter in their mud houses, it is perhaps not surprising that over 9000 succumb every year to snake-bites. This horrifying figure has to be seen in proper perspective. Death and serious injury come in a multitude of guises to the poor in India. For example, it was reported that whereas only four people in Bombay were hospitalized for snake-bites in one year, no fewer than 20,000 were admitted with serious rat-bites, most of them children bitten while sleeping. And, of course, neither snake-bites nor rat-bites can compare with the annual slaughter on

India's undisciplined roads, where, in spite of the relatively small number of vehicles, the death-rate is among the highest in the world. To quote a typical newspaper report of a traffic accident: 'Three of the occupants of the taxi were killed outright; the *seven other passengers* all suffered broken arms or legs'.

The general attitude towards snakes is ambivalent. Usually it is one of fear, yet few villagers willingly kill them. Cobras indeed are venerated in many parts of India. In Kerala, part of the village compound is often set aside for snake worship. At one religious festival a dozen Cobras may be extracted from their holes in the bunds around the paddyfields and after an elaborate ceremony of veneration carefully returned unharmed. The handlers are also apparently unharmed, although no attempt is made to remove or milk the poison fangs of the snakes. To a Western observer it is an astonishing demonstration of religious conviction.

Lizards of many species abound in the dry region and the attractive little spatula-toed geckos can be seen running about on the walls and ceilings even in town hotel bedrooms, where they feast on the abundant flies and moths. Some much larger geckos and agamids inhabit the tropical forests and deserts. One such species became very familiar to British troops in the Burmese jungle during the war, when its incessant nocturnal cry of 'tuck-too' infuriated exhausted men trying to sleep.

Strangely enough, although many Indian villagers regard snakes benevolently, some Moslems are terrified by harmless lizards, agamids and geckos. In Cholistan I was solemnly warned that the attractively marked little Leopard Gecko was so deadly that not only its bite but its breath could kill a man. The villagers became almost hysterical when we handled one for photography. A small and equally harmless skink (a type of legless lizard) was described as a dangerous snake with a head at each end. Another lizard was accused of climbing up the legs of buffaloes to steal their milk, a superstition similar to that attributed in Europe to a bird, the Nightjar, or Goatsucker as it used to be called.

Several species of big monitor lizards, some nearly two metres in length, can be seen in both tropical forest and desert regions. My own favourite is the Water Monitor, which is spangled with small yellow dots and has a long blue tongue which constantly flickers from its pink gape. It is a splendid sight basking on a log among the floating water hyacinths. An even more powerful creature is the fast-running Desert Monitor, which preys on rodents and birds in the Sind Desert. All the monitors, like the big snakes, have been constantly hunted by the skin-traders, who exported their skins in hundreds of thousands for making handbags and shoes. As a consequence, all five monitor species are now threatened and the export of their skins is prohibited.

Many different species of turtles can be seen around village ponds. Some grow to considerable size and are preyed upon by Jackals and other scavengers. In Nepal, Lammergeyer Vultures are known to pick them up and drop them on rocky ground in order to break their hard carapaces. It was probably one of these great birds which dropped a turtle on the head of the poet Aeschylus in Greece and killed him. In a pool in the Bayazid Bustami shrine in Chittagong there are nearly 300 turtles of venerable age and astonishing size, which are locally regarded as sacred. They are fed every day on raw cow's lung, in which the enterprising street traders do a brisk trade with visiting pilgrims to the shrine. I was amused by the indignation of the pilgrims when hungry Black Kites and Jungle Crows swooped down and snatched the dripping hunks of meat from their hands before they could be offered to the turtles. The species is unique and restricted to this one pond.

Throughout the world turtles are heavily exploited for their meat, eggs and carapaces or 'shells'. The State of Orissa, on India's east coast, has the distinction of preserving the breeding beaches of no fewer than 300,000 Olive Ridley Turtles, a species whose global status is endangered. There are also colonies of Olive Ridley and Green Turtles on the sand beaches of some other States. A few Hawksbill Turtles nest in southern Tamil Nadu, in the Sundarbans and on offshore islands. In Pakistan the Sind Wildlife Management Board, with initial help from the WWF, protects important breeding beaches of Green and Olive Ridley Turtles at Hawkes Bay and Sandspit, not far from Karachi. The local Pakistanis eat neither the eggs nor the meat of the turtles and their children have become enthusiastic helpers to the researchers that supervise the colonies.

The Threatened Environment

From the preceding pages it will be obvious that throughout the Indian subcontinent wildlife has suffered a very serious decline, due chiefly to the enormous reduction of forests and the steep increase in the human and livestock populations. Nevertheless, the variety of species of mammals, birds, reptiles and plants which can still be enjoyed is astonishingly great. Some substantial remnants of all the various forest types still remain and the scenic splendour of the subcontinent, although much altered, is still magnificent. Moreover, thanks to the lead given by the heads of State of all the countries concerned, and particularly the example set by the late Mrs Gandhi, there is now a firm and growing interest in the value of wildlife as a national heritage. Many State schools teach children to understand the importance of the natural world of living organisms and universities are increasingly producing graduates in environmental science and wildlife management. India now has nearly 490 national parks and sanctuaries covering over 4 per cent of its land surface. These are attracting increasing numbers not only of foreign tourists but also of local nationals. Protective legislation has been enacted and international agreements have been ratified for the protection of species and habitats. India, Nepal, Pakistan and Bangladesh are parties to the World Heritage Convention, which provides for the designation of areas of outstanding universal value as World Heritage sites, and all of these countries except Bangladesh have signed the Ramsar Convention, which is concerned with promoting the wise use of wetlands. They also participate in Unesco's programme for the establishment of a world-wide network of biosphere reserves. Bhutan, the least despoiled country and the one where wildlife has been least persecuted, has made an astonishing contribution by setting aside over 20 per cent of its territory as protected areas. Nepal now has eight excellent national parks, four wildlife reserves and one hunting reserve, covering nearly 8 per cent of the country. Pakistan's network of 95 national parks and wildlife sanctuaries covers almost 5 per cent of the country. Only in Bangladesh is the protected areas system grossly inadequate (less than one per cent) for the conservation of its rather more limited wildlife resources. It might easily be concluded from all this that the corner has been turned and that the future for wildlife is bright.

Alas, such a conclusion would be wildly optimistic. The natural environment of the subcontinent, on which all life, including man, depends, is continuing to deteriorate at an alarming rate. To understand the reasons for this it is necessary to examine its present state and to consider the interaction of the various causes. These have been analysed with great frankness in a series of *Citizens' Reports on The State of India's Environment* published first in 1982 and again in 1985 by the Centre for Science and Environment, a non-governmental organization based in New Delhi. Many of the statistics in the following pages are taken from these sources.

First and foremost is the fact that the pressure of human numbers on the land and natural resources is rapidly increasing. With a population expected to exceed one thousand million at the turn of the century, despite progress with birth control, it has been repeatedly argued that the population pressure has outstripped the country's capacity to cope. A UN study has shown, however, that India can feed two and a half times this projected population. The answer lies in proper soil and water management. Similarly, Bangladesh, one of the most densely populated countries in the world, has the potential to be self-supporting.

Both India and Pakistan have constructed major hydro-electric dams in order to provide increased energy and irrigation, but according to the *Citizens' Reports* the results have been little short of catastrophic as they were not planned or executed in consultation with either qualified soil scientists or ecologists. In consequence, one quarter of India's 40,000,000 hectares of canal-irrigated land is now suffering from serious water-logging and siltation. Most of the catchment areas have suffered a massive loss of topsoil and are turning into deserts which hundreds of thousands of peasant farmers have had to abandon. I saw clear evidence of this at the Kali River Dam in Karnataka and at the Tarbela Dam in Pakistan. The loss of tree-cover at Tarbela caused an annual loss of 400,000,000 tons of silt into the Indus River. Another ecological disaster is the Farraka Barrage in India. This is diverting upriver up to 40 per cent of the dry season flow of the Ganges, damaging the mangrove ecosystem of the Sundarbans in Bangladesh and disrupting the migrations of Hilsa, or Mountain Trout. Even long-established protected areas have not escaped the ambitious plans of the engineers, who did not hesitate to flood the Ramganga Valley in the beautiful Corbett National Park in the Siwalik Hills, thus depriving the wild Elephant population of its important feeding ground. Current controversial plans include the construction of dams in the Narmada Valley and at Tehri, a narrow Himalayan gorge in the headwaters of the Ganges. Both projects involve the displacement or endangerment of hundreds of thousands of people.

In India the amount of land subject to flooding has doubled in the last ten years. Dams which the engineers had calculated would be fully effective for 100 years are now expected to fail in only 30 or 40 years because of miscalculations of the rate of siltation. Corbett's Ramganga Dam, for example, is silting up four times faster than anticipated. Jawaharlal Nehru called India's dams 'the temples of modern India as testimonials to human toil and skill'. Toil, yes, but so far as skill is concerned this veneration must be judged against the penalties paid in rural areas, which have frequently far outweighed the value of the extra power generated.

It has been calculated that 53 per cent of India's land is now subject to serious degradation from erosion, waterlogging, salinity, alkalinity, or the ill-effects of shifting cultivation. Of these, flooding and excessive salinity are the chief problems and both can be attributed to inadequate control of the major rivers. Pollution is another very serious problem. No less than 70 per cent of all available freshwater sources in India are now polluted The use of chemical fertilizers and pesticides is encouraged by the government. But the factories discharge their untreated effluents into the rivers and the payment of subsidies encourages the overdosing of crops, so that run-off quickly pollutes the irrigation channels. The factories are all too often located close to big towns where labour is readily available, the consequence of which was demonstrated by the tragedy at Bhopal in 1984, where 2500 inhabitants were killed by a gas leakage from a Union Carbide factory. The multi-national chemical companies of the United States and Europe, where lethal and persistent products such as DDT, Aldrin and BHC are now banned by law, still cynically export them to the Third World and great quantities of them are used in the Indian subcontinent. Sulphur-dioxide and oxides of nitrogen as a fall-out from factory chimneys in the form of 'acid rain' is also damaging public health, forests and treasured buildings such as the Taj Mahal, where recent precautionary measures are now proving effective. Many once famous sand beaches of India, which represented potential sources of wealth from tourism, are now hopelessly spoiled by the back-wash of industrial pollutants and human excreta. Even India's first marine national park on the Gulf of Kutch, which was once a paradise for marine life, is threatened by effluents and oil spillage.

The greatest cause of pollution, however, is not inorganic chemicals but the fact that one third of India's town dwellers and 99 per cent of its rural population have no sanitary facilities whatever. Out of 3119 towns and cities, only eight have fully adequate sewerage systems. A *Citizens' Report* states that human waste accounts for four times as much water pollution as all the industrial and agricultural effluents combined. It quotes the example of the Yamuna River. Before this river enters Delhi (which quadrupled its population in only 20 years) it is reasonably pure, with only 7500 coliform organisms per 100 millilitres of water. Below Delhi it contains 24 million per 100 millilitres, and is nothing but a lifeless sewer covered with dead fish. Water-borne diseases such as dysentery, typhoid, jaundice, cholera, filariasis and guinea-worm are rampant and many are actually increasing. Three children die from such diseases or from malnutrition in India every minute. Mosquitoes and sandflies have bred immunity to the government's massive use of DDT spraying and in consequence the scourge malaria has again increased sharply during the past decade. A national programme aimed ultimately at a complete sewerage system is now under way, but already fears are expressed that although this will help city dwellers it is very unlikely to alleviate the problem in rural areas where the great majority of the population lives.

Outsiders who know and love India, as I do, are always puzzled by the difference between the insistence, at all levels of society, on the scrupulous daily ablutions of the body and the almost total lack of concern about the disposal of human excreta. Our Western preoccupation with hygiene is looked upon as not only ridiculously fastidious, but as uneconomic, if not barbarous. Every day throughout most of Asia hundreds of millions of people squat unconcernedly to defecate at the roadside and in the paddyfields as their ancestors have always done. The village pond serves not only for bathing, washing clothes and watering cattle, but in innumerable cases also as a source of water for drinking and cooking – and as a cess-pit for the spread of disease. Drinking-water from a stand-pipe is available in a very small percentage of villages, but it functions only erratically and sometimes not at all.

India has 242,000,000 domestic cattle including buffaloes, and 117,000,000 goats and sheep. Less than a quarter of the manure they produce goes back to the land. The rest is dried and burnt as fuel. Yet, above all, the land cries out for organic fertilization. Millions of tons of water hyacinths choke every village pond and 4,000,000 hectares of India's waterways. These beautiful but invasive plants were introduced from South America and are capable of multiplying 60,000 times in only eight months. They offer a limitless source of free fertilizer but remain unused except for making paper, or for feeding pigs, which are surely misplaced priorities. India's farmers rarely plough back either manure or vegetable waste from crops, yet their crops deplete the soil of nearly 18,000,000 tons of plant nutrients every year, so the land inevitably becomes steadily less productive. Even though the farmers may realize this, the pernicious practice by the land-

The dam constructed on the Ramganga river has had a drastic impact on the wildlife in Corbett National Park. Besides drowning a large area of forest, it has dislocated the migratory route of elephant herds.

owners of moving their tenants from area to area on a share-cropping basis is sufficient to kill any interest in soil improvement. Even in Punjab, once famous as 'the green revolution State' which achieved the highest yield of wheat in the subcontinent, too much is being taken out of the soil and too little is put back. Today Punjab is listed as having one of the lowest levels of plant nutrients in its land, yet 5,000,000 tons of nutrient-rich rice straw are burnt there every year, instead of being ploughed back.

The fact that cows are sacred to Hindus poses yet another problem. Nearly all of them are emaciated and disease ridden, but on religious grounds may not be culled. Millions of them forage for what they can find in the forests, deserts or city streets, where they cause countless accidents. Motorists who run into them risk a lynching. As beef is 'unclean' to so many, their value to the national economy is in any case very small. Nehru, who knew the weaknesses of the Indian character better than anyone, said:

'In India there is a difference between precept and practice. In no country is life valued in theory so much as in India and many people hesitate to destroy even the meanest or most harmful of animals. But in practice we ignore the animal world. We grow excited about the protection of the cow... But we imagine we have done our duty by passing some legislation. This results not in the protection of the cow but in much harm to it as well as to human beings. The cattle are let loose and deteriorate, so that the very purpose for which we value them is defeated.'

This confusion between precept and practice is at the root of many of India's problems. The government is unquestionably humanitarian and strives mightily to improve the lot of its people. India's scientists are among the best in the world and there is certainly no lack of knowledge either of what is wrong, or of the means by which improvements could be made. Yet again and again priorities seem to be muddled and the fulfilment of admirable plans gets lost or diverted in the world's largest and most pervasive bureaucracy. Although the need for improved sanitation and wiser land-use policies is everywhere admitted, priority was given to high-profile schemes such as the costly development of the atomic bomb, which most people believe few countries needed less than India.

The plight of the rural population, of which 350 million are living at below the recognized subsistence level, is obvious to all, but it is usually the comparatively well-off city dwellers who most benefit from government policies. India rightly takes pride in its claim to be the world's greatest democracy, but so long as the caste system persists, with its pernicious effects on political, social and economic life, it is difficult to see how the difference between precept and practice will ever be overcome. For all the government's benevolent intentions, to the peasant farmer even the lowliest official has a terrifying, almost god-like power over his existence. Every villager is acutely aware that unless he has the means to bribe an official his complaints will never be heard, let alone be considered or noted for action.

When Mahatma Gandhi promised that there would be no high class and no low class in India he was wildly applauded. Yet decades later the caste system can still be seen at every level of society. Very few Westerners can comprehend its intricate ramifications, or the depth of the conviction which sustains it. The cultured Brahmin who feels polluted if touched by an 'untouchable', suffers from it just as much as the poorest vagrant who is forbidden the use of the village well and must drink at the

The beautiful yet pernicious water hyacinth, Eichornia crassipes, *is the scourge of fresh-water systems throughout the subcontinent.*

cattle pond. Voluntary efforts to improve the lot of the landless and illiterate 'scheduled people' are still often resented by villagers, on the grounds that the destitute should not be encouraged to compete with their betters. Local courts have frequently supported this view. The in-bred, patient acceptance of the caste system, which the Mahatma tried so hard to break, is something which village co-operatives and well-meaning government relief programmes for the poor can alleviate, but the problem itself remains intractable. India remains firmly compartmentalized by caste and religion.

So far as the natural environment is concerned, it is not too late to reverse many of the adverse trends from which the subcontinent is suffering. Legislation already exists for the control of pollution, although it is rarely implemented. Europe and America have demonstrated that it is possible to restore the purity of water sources by the strict enforcement of such legislation. It would be possible to restore the soil fertility of many agricultural areas if the huge resources of organic waste and animal manure were ploughed back instead of going up in smoke and if erosion by wind and water were better controlled. Techniques now exist for halting the disastrous spread of deserts, many of which in Pakistan and north-west India were once forested. The degradation of forest s by fuel gatherers could be alleviated if governments developed and subsidized efficient bio-gas cookers for rural villages and ensured that supplies of wet cattle dung were equitably shared to fuel them. In 1982 fewer than 20,000 such cookers existed in India (compared with 7,000,000 in China) and unless a family owned five or more cows it had insufficient manure to produce any methane gas for the cooker. Only 10 per cent of the rural poor own as many cattle as this, so the cookers failed to get the support they deserved. There is also ample waste-land available for planting quick-growing trees to supplement fuel and building supplies, if this were done on a large enough scale and under government subsidy with the active co-operation of rural villages. A notably successful example of this already exists in Gujarat State and there is certainly no lack of expertise in India's very efficient Forest Department.

A considerable variation in the attitudes of State Governments towards matters such as these made it difficult to bring about the coherent national conservation strategy for which Mrs Gandhi was striving. Nevertheless some notable progress has been made. For example, in order to control the increasing losses of forested areas, which between 1950 and 1980 had amounted to 4,300,000 hectares, the Forest (Conservation) Act of 1980 was introduced. This immediately prevented any State Government or other authority from diverting forest land to non-forestry purposes without the prior consent of the Central Government. Although considered controversial at the time, this Act proved highly beneficial and the annual rate of conversion of forests dropped from about 140,000 hectares pre-1980 to about 6500 hectares in the 1980s.

India has less than 20 per cent of its original forests left; Bangladesh has a mere 7 per cent, while only 5 per cent of Pakistan's huge land is forested. Between 1951 and 1980 some 4,100,000 hectares of native forest were felled in India, mainly for agriculture, and by 1982 the rate of loss had accelerated to more than a million hectares a year including bamboo and mangrove forests. Some extensive replanting is, of course, being done, but most of this is of commercial tree species which do not provide the fruit, nuts, foliage, resins and thatching which are so essential to forest tribes as well as to wildlife. Between 1950 and 1980, the total area of replanting amounted to 3,550,000 hectares, but less than 20 per cent of this was intended for soil or moisture conservation. In Bihar State, where owing to failure in communication tribal people resisted the government policy of replacing virgin forest with commercial trees, there was serious rioting, resulting in 13 deaths and 200 arrests. The government failed to recognize that the great majority of its millions of primitive tribal people are totally dependent on the produce of the natural forest for their livelihood. A major initiative was launched in 1985 with the establishment of the National Wastelands Board, whose principal role is to bring degraded lands under productive use through a massive programme of reafforestation.

That grass-root support for environmental reform concerning the use of forests would be forthcoming from the rural population has been demonstrated by the success of the Chipko Andolan movement. Beginning in the Garhwal Himalayas as a local tree-hugging protest against the destruction of natural forests, this has developed into a national campaign that has been internationally acclaimed. The movement has been successful in forcing bans on felling in the Himalayan forests of Uttar Pradesh above 1000 metres, in the Western Ghats and in the Vindhyas. Native tree-planting campaigns led by the Chipko women have often achieved a much higher success rate of both survival and growth than in the neighbouring government-controlled monoculture plantations.

Sufficient expertise exists in the world to make safer and more productive use of the subcontinent's ample resources of water. According to the FAO, even Bangladesh could be made self-supporting in food if its irrigation and agriculture were modernized. But mechanized farming is not the answer. This benefits only the large land-owner and deprives the poor of their traditional labour-intensive employment as weeders, reapers and threshers of cereal crops. Foreign aid should be concentrated on encouraging self-help and on providing expertise to improve the use of local resources, rather than on the present export of government-subsidized surplus grain from the West. Whether such reforms take place will depend largely on the wisdom of the governments concerned. But also on the manner in which the Foreign Aid Programmes of the Western governments are devised. At present most of them are far from altruistic in their insistence on a quid pro quo. 'I'll send you grain if you will buy my tractors,' is scarcely humanitarian. The United Nations, the World Bank and the International Monetary Fund are at last trying to overcome this horse-trading attitude which inflicts such unnecessary hardship on recipient countries. At the United Nations the environmental crisis which threatens the subcontinent is very fully documented. What is lacking is the political will to take the necessary action while there is yet time to avert catastrophe.

Mrs Gandhi declared that India must stand on its own feet, by which she meant that it must solve its own problems and not depend on foreign aid. This brave posture deserves commendation. A similar determination can be seen in Nepal, which is one of the poorest nations in the world and heavily dependent on its natural resources for survival. No less than 87 per cent of its energy resources are provided by burning wood from its forests. The resultant massive deforestation has led to serious erosion and flooding, which affects not only Nepal but also India and Bangladesh. Recognizing that the process of development and management of the environment are inextricably linked, HM Government of Nepal invited the World Conservation Union (IUCN) to help formulate a National Conservation Strategy. This was completed in 1987 and endorsed as government policy the following year. Nepal is one of the first countries to have responded so whole-heartedly to the recommendations of the World Conservation Strategy, which was launched in 1980 by IUCN, WWF and the United Nations Environment Programme (UNEP). By adopting a policy of inter-sectoral co-operation, particularly with respect to developments that have a bearing on the fate of the natural environment, Nepal is setting an example to the world. Although most nations now take environmental matters seriously, even the United Kingdom and the United States still suffer from the competing ambitions of their various government ministries. If a problem happens to have a bearing on the short-term national economy it is usually this factor rather than the environmental consequence which has the ultimate sanction. Only the adoption of a firmly held and fully co-ordinated national conservation strategy can overcome such conflicts.

So far as the future for wildlife in the Indian subcontinent is concerned, I have nothing but admiration for the measures already taken in the face of such overpowering local problems. Even Afghanistan, which I last visited with HRH The Duke of Edinburgh on behalf of the WWF just before the Russian invasion, had by then created several wildlife reserves. Whether in the long term the measures taken in the subcontinent will remain effective will, I believe, depend on what Indian experts are already calling a better understanding of the human dimension in wildlife management. By this they mean the integration of local people into the conservation planning, by identifying wildlife and wilderness areas as essential elements of a resource system in a socio-economic sense. Unless this can be achieved there is a danger that the conservation of wildlife will increasingly be regarded as putting the welfare of wild animals before that of people. In countries where a great percentage of the population lives at mere subsistence level it is to be expected that such antagonism could easily arise.

Some valuable studies have been conducted in India by comparing two different methods of handling the human equation when setting up protected areas. One was at the Gir National Park in Gujarat, the other at the Palamau Reserve complex in Bihar. In the former it was decided to remove all the Maldhari villagers and their cattle and resettle them beyond the park boundaries. They were given fresh, unpolluted land which was ploughed at government expense. Free transportation, essential building and agricultural equipment, water resources, a school and a community centre were provided. The re-location was highly successful and achieved without social protest. The cost was less than US $250 a head, plus a similar amount as a loan for house-building. As described earlier in this book, the effect of the removal of the Maldharis and their huge herds of cattle was immediately apparent in the park. With the recovery of the vegetation and the sowing of the old village sites with native grasses, the populations of deer and other animals quickly recovered. Nevertheless, the operation, although so successfully handled, did nothing to interest the villagers in the conservation objectives, nor to integrate them in the project in a socio-economic sense.

At Palamau a different approach was used. A fully protected core area for wildlife was established as a national park, but the tribal Bihari villagers were permitted, within certain limits, to remain in the substantial sanctuary buffering the park. In this buffer zone they continued to graze their cattle and to harvest controlled quantities of their traditional necessities such as bamboo, thatching grass, wood fuel and wild fruit, roots and tubers for food. A limited amount of shifting cultivation in marginal areas was also permitted. Moreover, the tribal people were employed in the construction of patrol roads, guard huts, watch towers, fire-breaks and other necessary work in the protected areas complex. Their interest in the conservation programme became obvious and they benefited from the additional water sources which were developed for the wildlife. By this integration into the management planning, both goodwill and sustained and active co-operation were obtained and all social disruption avoided.

The Indian Ministry of Environment and Forests has these and similar case histories on which to base future planning. It would appear that the full integration of often illiterate tribal people into the conservation effort is not only desirable but completely achievable. Provisions are made for this in the new National Forest Policy, which should go far in overcoming the threat of a man versus animal conflict. In this respect India has again pioneered an admirable example to the rest of Asia.

I have always been fascinated by my occasional contacts with the aboriginal tribes which I have met in Asia, South America, Australasia and Central Africa. Unlike other societies, they have learned to live in easy equilibrium with the natural world; their reliance on the resources of the forests or deserts which they inhabit is always deeply impressive. Such people are completely remote, having absolutely nothing in common with the Western world. The forest tribes of India are no exception. Everything they need for survival is found in the bountiful forests and forest streams. There are ample sources of food, bamboos for building, palm leaves for thatching, vines for binding and they know of countless medicinal plants for their ailments. They never plunder or abuse the rich generosity of the forests, nor kill any living thing wantonly.

Now many of the Indian forest tribes are being dispossessed by the felling of their forests and are being driven out into the alien world of officialdom, incomprehensible laws and customs which frighten them. Unable to cope with the traumatic confusion of the twentieth century, they are deeply unhappy. What, for example, is to become of the 75,000 tribals, 40,000 of them Madia Gonds, who are being dispossessed of their land in order that hydro-electric installations may be built on the Godavari River? Or the displaced Cholanaickans of Kerala State who have taken to a troglodyte existence, to the embarrassment of local officials who find them almost impossible to assimilate? The future of the 'Scheduled Tribes', as they are called, poses many problems for the government and as they number some 44,000,000 throughout India, there are no easy answers.

Throughout its long history, India has demonstrated its genius for quietly assimilating many widely differing peoples, and unique skill in overcoming the seemingly insurmountable social problems which some have temporarily caused. A part of the tribal population has already been educated and some have even occupied positions of responsibility in local government. It will take time to assimilate the remainder, but time has always been on India's side. All the past assimilations have enriched the nation's culture and the Scheduled Tribes will undoubtedly make their contribution. It is already recognized that the forest tribals have unique knowledge and skill in the use of medicinal plants, which can benefit not only India but the world at large.

The natural world of the Indian subcontinent is now at the crossroads. Either the governments of the countries concerned will recognize the reality of the present threats tot he environment and make a concerted effort to overcome them, or they will have to face the loss of much of their natural heritage and increasing hardship for their people. Almost all the causes of the sickness from which the environment is suffering have had their counterparts in other countries. They have been studied in depth and have been fully documented by experts of many nations. Scientists in India and its neighbouring countries are fully alive to the need for urgent action, as has been demonstrated by the conclusions expressed in the *Citizens' Reports*. Their findings echo those relating to the region in the *Global 2000 Report*, a world-wide environmental survey commissioned by former President Jimmy Carter and prepared by a team of distinguished specialists. There is no mystery about the nature of the reforms needed to arrest the present adverse trends, which are making Man himself an endangered species. Two things are required. First, fully co-ordinated national conservation strategies which combine eco-development on a sustained-yield basis with long-term objectives for agriculture, forestry, industry, public health and population control. Second, a new set of planning and financial priorities, which place the welfare of the natural environment and people above all considerations. Both

A Malasar tribal village in the heart of the Anamalai Sanctuary in the Western Ghats. Tribes in India have traditionally lived in close harmony with the indigenous forests, and any threat to this vulnerable environment poses a consequential threat to their whole way of life.

require great political determination. It is, of course, easy enough to suggest solutions, but to implement them is another matter. To create the necessary governmental infra-structure alone is a daunting task.

Almost unique in the world is the Indian Constitution, which lays down as a principle of state policy that 'it shall be the duty of every citizen . . . to protect and improve the natural environment, including forests, lakes, rivers and wildlife and to have compassion for all living creatures'. But as the situation worsens, the government has become passive, with only a few officers and non-governmental organizations taking an active role. The Indian Board for Wildlife, which advises both Central and State Governments on matters relating to conservation, did not meet between 1987 and 1996. There are, however, some notable achievements. The Wild Life (Protection) Act, passed in 1972 and amended in 1991, provides a central legal framework for the establishment of protected areas, and for controlling hunting and all trade in wildlife and wildlife products.; in 1973 'Project Tiger' was implemented. This has led to the creation of 23 protected reserves totalling 31,000 square kilometres. Although originally regarded as a single-species project, it is in effect a total ecosystem

preservation which benefits all forms of wildlife and is one of the most successful ever executed by any country. In 1976 a Directorate of Wildlife Education and Research was established, providing post-graduate diploma courses in wildlife management. This was followed by the creation of the Wildlife Institute of India in 1982, which has established a strong professional and scientific base for conservation.

Unlike many prominent nations, India has ratified all the main international conservation conventions: the Convention on International Trade in Endangered Species of Flora and Fauna (CITES); the Convention on Wetlands of International Importance (the Ramsar Convention); the Convention on Migratory Species of Wild Animas (the Migratory Species Convention) and the International Convention for the Regulation of Whaling (the

During construction of Karnataka's Kabini dam, Kurba tribals were translocated from their valley settlements to regions close by, where large tracts of indigenous forest were cleared for their benefit. Destruction of forests in the subcontinent today poses a serious ecological threat to the whole environment.

Whaling Convention). The driving force behind these initiatives was the indefatigable Indira Gandhi. She played a leading role in the launching of the World Conservation Strategy in Stockholm and immediately introduced it in India. The basic theme of India's eighth Five-Year Plan is sustainable development. It was decided that during the first half of the 1990s the emphasis was to be on evaluating and conserving natural resources, controlling pollution, and rehabilitating rivers and wastelands. In 1988 a plan for a national network of 651 protected areas, covering 4.6 per cent of the country, was formulated, but few such areas have been adopted. Improving the effectiveness with which protected areas are managed is a high priority.

The natural world is the result of millions of years of infinitely gradual evolution, which in the Indian subcontinent was abundantly expressed in terms of scenic splendour and variety of living organisms at the turn of the twentieth century. The decline which became apparent by the middle of the century is now becoming rapidly steeper. Ever year that passes sees more irreparable losses which make salvation more difficult. Future generations will not forgive us if this magnificent world heritage is not saved for posterity. It is not sufficient merely to hope that it will somehow be saved by local initiative. It is part of our threatened world and its fate is our fate.

It will be said, with justice, that someone from the West, which consumes four-fifths of the natural resources of the world, has no right to criticise policies or conditions in the Indian subcontinent. It is, however, certainly not by right but with humility and I hope with objectivity that my views, as seen through Western eyes, are expressed. I can only hope that my friends in the various countries concerned will understand my anxiety, as a conservationist, about the future for a part of the world for whose gentle and long-suffering people I have unbounded admiration.

THE HIMALAYAS
The Edge of the Roof of the World

In the intense, sub-zero silence of the sky at an altitude of 9000 metres, a solitary Himalayan Griffon Vulture rides the wind. Far below, between the shreds of cloud blown like smoke among the high peaks, it can see the glistening ice slopes, plunging to the chaotically shattered lips of the glaciers. Below them again sprawl the vast stony barrens, where Marmots pop in and out of their burrows and Snow Partridges scratch for fallen seed among the rocks.

The barrens in turn fall away southwards to the stunted birches, then the taller conifers, and finally the deep gorges, dark with rhododendron forest, where a thousand streams cascade downs the rocks. Only a few kilometres beyond that, as the altitude diminishes, the Nepalese foothills give way to the vivid green of the semi-tropical terai and then the luxuriant and humid tropical deciduous jungle of the Indian States of Uttar Pradesh and Bihar.

The transition through so many different climatic and vegetational zones over a distance of less than a hundred kilometres is dramatic. To the north of the Himalayas is the immense and inhospitable Tibetan Plateau, but to the east and west, in an unbroken succession of snowy peaks, the Himalayan range extends for 3500 kilometres, at either end curving southwards towards Afghanistan and Burma. With 50 mountain peaks exceeding 7600 metres in altitude, they form one of the world's greatest mountain chains. Soaring above them is Mount Everest, or Sagarmatha, Goddess Mother of the World, as the Nepalese call it, with a height of 8848 metres. The only passes through this barrier, the ancient trade routes to the icy, windswept roof of the world in the Tibetan Autonomous Region and China, involve climbing to an altitude of at least 5500 metres.

The Himalayas form a weather barrier which is responsible for India's monsoon climate. Three of the world's greatest rivers, the Indus, the Ganges and the Brahmaputra, rise among its peaks and flow southward to water the heat-stricken northern plains of Pakistan and India, where 15 per cent of the world's population depends heavily upon them for survival.

The alpine region of the Himalayas abounds with colourful flowers of incomparable beauty. The famous Valley of Flowers in the Garhwal Himalayas affords an easy means of seeing them. The stony alpine regions of the Himalayas above the tree-line are carpeted in spring with colourful cushions of blue gentians and starred with saxifrages, asters, anemones, primulas, fritillarias and yellow edelweiss. Junipers and buckthorns cling to the stony slopes.

Lower down, in the sub-alpine forests of birch and conifers, are immense thickets of rhododendrons, some growing up to 15 metres high. Among them are laurels, huge white magnolias, pink daphnes, azaleas, various lilies and the famous blue, yellow and crimson Himalayan poppies. Fragrant white Himalayan musk roses climb to the tops of the trees.

Up above the tree-line, only the occasional accumulated litter of a climbers' camp defaces the scene – evidence that man has dared to challenge the heights. Below, the presence of man is more evident. Here and there are isolated Buddhist monasteries with their picturesque stupas and fluttering white prayer flags, and Hindu temples, many dedicated to Shiva – the 'destroyer' of the Hindu faith. Then come the Sherpa villages, where shaggy yaks shelter in the lower rooms of snug, stone-built houses. Increasingly, the natural vegetation has been lopped for fuel or removed to make way for cultivation. Even the spectacular Sagarmatha National Park has its legacy of trees that have been mutilated by trekking parties.

In the 14 years prior to 1978, Nepal lost nearly 6 per cent of its total forest area. Its forests are still diminishing due to domestic fuel, fodder and timber requirements, but at a slower rate. Of greater concern is the deterioration in the quality of Nepal's forests as they are opened up by selective felling and lopping. About 37 per cent of Nepal's geographic area is at least partially covered in trees and shrubs but some of this is in poor condition. Most of the foothills have been stripped bare and everywhere there are intricate terraces, created by superhuman effort, for the growing of rice, millet, barley, maize and potatoes. Potatoes are grown by the Sherpas of Nepal up to an altitude of about 4500 metres. However, many of the centuries-old terraces have long ago been eroded and abandoned because of the loss of the stabilizing tree-cover. From the air the sheer extent of this monument to the frailty of human endeavour is a saddening if fascinating sight. The loss of trees has resulted in many landslides, some of which have destroyed whole villages. The higher the terracing, the greater the landslides.

Despite the losses, however, there is still a wealth of interest for the botanist. In a single day more than a hundred species of birds can be seen. Such spectacular animals as Snow Leopards, Black Bears, Red Pandas and various mountain sheep and goats roam the heights of Gilgit, Hunza, Ladakh, Nepal, Sikkim and Bhutan. Although hunters of many nations have taken a heavy toll of these animals in the past, the governments of all the Himalayan countries have in recent years made strenuous efforts to protect them.

A chain of National Parks and Wildlife Sanctuaries now stretches from the Khunjerab in Pakistan, past the superb Sagarmatha National Park surrounding Everest, to the protected areas of Sikkim, Bhutan and Assam, where mountain wildlife and stupendous scenery can be enjoyed to the full. Access to those at high altitudes is limited by snowy conditions, but the others are readily accessible in the dry season and some provide facilities for visitors. To see them is to enjoy the experience of a lifetime, but whereas there was once a long slow trek up from the Indian plains, the modern traveller, arriving by air, may take some time to acclimatize to the high altitudes. The little Momblasa, or Everest View Lodge at Khumjung, perched high above the Sherpa village of Namche Bazar and the Dudh Kosi gorge, has oxygen masks available in every bedroom. The hotel balconies offer quite magnificent panoramic views of the peaks of Everest, Lhotse, Nuptse and Ama Dablam. Tourists who have made the trip by helicopter direct from Kathmandu often have to go straight to bed with an oxygen mask, missing the chance to enjoy their surroundings. However, this can be avoided by trekking in easy stages from Kathmandu, by way of Namche, up to the 4000 metre altitude of the lodge.

Above: The arid slopes of the Karakoram range rise above the fertile strip that borders the upper Indus.

Far left: Bharal, or Blue Sheep, in typical semi-desert habitat on mountain slopes, high above the Shang valley in Ladakh. Bharal are also found in the high, windswept barrens of Tibet, Nepal and Sikkim. In summer they live at altitudes of up to 5500 metres, descending to about 3500 metres in winter. A member of the goat-antelope sub-family, their horns are smooth and swept back like those of a goat, although the rams are not bearded. A Bharal climbs with goat-like agility, but its flocks graze like sheep – invariably on open slopes, and avoiding bushy or forested areas. Bharal are extremely alert and difficult to approach. They are preyed upon by Snow Leopards (see page 36), which lie in wait for them among the rocks.

Left: An immature Bharal ram. When adult, its horns will sweep backwards in a semi-circle. The slate-grey coloration provides splendid camouflage on rocky mountain slopes.

Right: Although the Himalayan peaks in Ladakh are not as high as in Nepal, they are still awe-inspiring. The mountains are equally rugged, with similarly immense glaciers descending their slopes from the high snow fields. (Left and right foreground.) In summer their melting waters create spectacular waterfalls which cascade into the valleys far below. The Himalayan range is about 3500 kilometres long and 200 kilometres wide, forming an almost impregnable barrier between the Indian subcontinent and China. The main system comprises three parallel ranges: the Outer Himalaya flanking the Indo-Gangetic plain; the Middle Himalaya, locally represented by the Fir Panjal in Kashmir, Dhaula Dhar in Himachal Pradesh and Mahabharat Lekh in Nepal; and the Great Himalaya which lies along the edge of the Tibetan Plateau at an average height of 5100 metres. The Himalayas are the youngest mountains in the subcontinent and were formed by a violent crumbling and up-thrust of the earth's crust along the edge of the Central Asian tableland, beginning in the late Cretaceous and early Tertiary periods. They are still rising and moving northwards under the pressure of the Indian peninsula, which once formed part of Gondwanaland before drifting on the earth's molten crust to join the Asian land mass. The animal life of the Himalayas is specially adapted to the fierce winds and extreme cold of the high altitudes. All the mammals have undercoats of dense fur and their feet are well adapted to travel through snow and over ice-clad rocks. The Yak's long, woolly coat and bushy tail, which reach almost to the ground, help to keep its feet warm in winter. Some of the small animals such as Marmots and Mouse Hares, which live as high as 5500 metres, store food in their burrows and, like the bears, go into a state of hibernation in the coldest weather. Other animals, such as Goral and Sambar, descend to the tree line. Langur Monkeys have been recorded as high as 4270 metres, and even Tigers have left their tracks in the snow at nearly 4000 metres. Some birds, such as Snow Finches and the hardy Snow Partridge, spend almost their entire lives at or above the snow line, and some even nest in the intense cold at 5000 metres.

Right: The Snow Leopard is one of the most elusive animals in the world. An inhabitant of the high peaks, plateaux and snow fields, it is widely but thinly distributed across the Himalayan massif.

Left: The Suru Valley in Ladakh. Still above the tree line, but here the stony slope is green with alpine vegetation. Above it rise the twin peaks of Nun (7725 m) and Kun (7672 m).

Right and far right: Colonies of Himalayan Marmots occupy the rocky slopes at very high altitudes, making their homes in burrows which give these perky animals some protection from the eagles which prey upon them. Ever-watchful, they stand on their hind legs and warn their fellows with a shrill whistling cry of alarm.

Right: A ribbon of green at the valley bottom contrasts with the barren sandstone slopes above.

Far right: A newly hatched Robin Accentor in its nest, in a low bush at 5100 metres in Ladakh. This high-altitude breeder survives intense cold.

Centre right: Flowers of *Pedicularis longifolia* growing at 4000 metres.

Full moon over the Karakoram mountains.

Top: The brilliantly coloured Monal, or Impeyan Pheasant, the most commonly seen of the Himalayan pheasants. Other species are rare due to hunting and loss of habitat. A programme to reintroduce the Cheer Pheasant to the Margalla Hills National Park in Pakistan, supported by the World Pheasant Association, has failed to re-establish them.

Above: The butterfly *Argymnis hyperbius*.

Left: The Common Kingfisher, one of nearly 20 different species of kingfisher found in the Indian subcontinent.

Above: The delicately tinted water lily, *Nelumbo nucifera*, growing on the edges of the Nagin Lake in Kashmir, one of the many lakes which make this one of the most beautiful States of India. These lakes are important for wildlife, for elsewhere many lakes and marshes have been polluted or drained for land reclamation.

Above: The Hangul or Kashmir Stag, one of India's endangered deer species, is related to the European Red Deer. These are young males. but a fully-grown stag can weigh 180 kilograms and bear antlers with as many as 14 points. Their numbers fell from an estimated 3000–5000 at the turn of the century to 140–170 in 1970. By the mid-1980s, the population had increased to an estimated 550, its recovery due to effective control of poaching and grazing by livestock. This population occurs in Dachigam National Park and occasionally frequents the nearby Kishtwat National Park.

Right: A wild Delphinium, *Delphinium himalyense.*

Top: Hangul hinds. These stately deer can best be seen in Dachigam National Park in Kashmir.

Above: A Holly Blue, or Hedge Blue Butterfly, one of the *Lycaenopsina*.

Left: Himalayan Ibex, occurring at high altitudes from Himachal Pradesh to Afghanistan in the Western Himalayas, are noted for their massive, scimitar-shaped horns, which can reach a length of more than one metre. (The record is 147 centimetres.) They usually live in herds of 10 to 50, with a sentinel always alert. At the sound of its whistling alarm, the herd dashes off at great speed, rushing up or down steep cliffs with astonishing agility.

Top left and right: Both Brown Bear and Black Bear can be seen in Dachigam National Park. The Himalayan Black Bear (left) is a very powerful animal, the males weighing up to 180 kilograms and sometimes growing up to two metres tall. Its glossy black fur, with a striking white 'V' across its chest, distinguishes it from the Brown Bear (right) and from the Sloth Bear (page 195) – which has a less distinctive 'V' on its shaggy fur. The Black Bear is found throughout the forested slopes of the Himalayas and eastward to Japan. It seldom ventures far above the tree line, usually hibernating in winter though some individuals may be active. It is a much more aggressive animal than the Brown Bear, which occurs in the sub-alpine and alpine zones, generally above the Black Bear's range. The Brown Bear avoids humans, but the Black Bear is renowned for raiding crops and attacking villagers if confronted. Both bears are very partial to the honey of wild bees.

Far left: The Indian Red Admiral butterfly *Vanessa indica*.

Far right: Wild raspberries – another favourite with the sweet-toothed bears.

Top left and right: Fungi of innumerable kinds play an important role in helping to break down the litter on the forest floor and return its nutrients to the soil. On the left is the toadstool *Coprinus disseminatus*, on the right the curious *Geastrum triplex*.

Above: Chukar Partridges in Dachigam National Park in Kashmir. They inhabit the drier regions of the Western Himalayas as far east as Central Nepal, generally at altitudes of 2100–4000 metres. Villagers often use them at festivals as substitutes for fighting cocks.

The Valley of Flowers in the Garhwal Himalaya of Uttar Pradesh is now well protected as a National Park. This paradise for botanists has become a major tourist attraction, enabling people to see the fantastic floral profusion of the lower mountain slopes. High in the valley, the flowering shrub *Polygonum polystachya*, (in the foreground), is growing at an altitude of 3500 metres.

The famous Himalayan Blue Poppy *Meconopsis aculeata*, which is now a favourite garden plant in Europe. Yellow and scarlet poppies also grown in the Himalayas.

The deep gorges in the Kedarnath Sanctuary provide some fine examples of unexploited broad-leaved mixed forests in the Himalayas.

49

Right: An ice bridge formed by a waterfall in the Garhwal Himalayas.

Left and far left: The Musk Deer, a primitive ruminant and not a true deer, is probably the most exploited animal of the Himalayan region. Thousands are killed every year for the male's 'musk pod', a sexual gland which lies beneath the skin of its abdomen and produces the distinctively scented secretion known as musk. Both males and females are shot and snared indiscriminately. The pods are used as a basis for perfumes, and for medicinal purposes throughout Asia. Japan represents the biggest international market, with pods fetching up to four times their weight in gold. Although the Musk Deer is now protected in the subcontinent, this illicit 'merchandise' is still smuggled out of Nepal and India. These inoffensive little creatures (they stand only 50 centimetres at the shoulder) live in the birch and rhododendron thickets near the tree line. Their large, splayed hooves prevent them from sinking too deep in soft snow. In the absence of horns, their long, projecting canine teeth are used for defence. During the day they lie hidden, coming out at dusk to feed. Unlike many deer, they live singly or in pairs.

Above: The brilliant flower of *Potentilla nepalensis*.

Left: Near the headwaters of the Alaknanda is the sacred Hemkund glacial lake, to which thousands of Sikhs and Hindus from all over India make an arduous pilgrimage on foot during the summer months (June-October). During the rest of the year, the snows make the lake inaccessible.

Overleaf: One of the most colourful flowers to be seen in the Valley of Flowers – a mass of *Impatiens sulcata*.

Mount Annapurna (8078 metres) in late afternoon sunlight.

The expanded hood of the Spectacled Cobra (far left), identified by the characteristic mark on the back of the hood, and the sheathed flower of the Snake Lily, *Arisaema nepenthoides* (left), display a striking resemblance. Three kinds of cobra occur in India: the Spectacled Cobra, the Monocled Cobra and the Black Cobra. The much larger King Cobra, or Hamadryad, is a different genus and occurs mainly in the tropical rain forests of south-western and north-eastern India. Although the cobra's venomous bite can be fatal to humans, these snakes play an important role in helping to control the vast population of rats and other rodents which annually consume thousands of tons of India's stored grain. In some parts of the country shrines are erected for the worship of cobras, which are pulled out of their holes and venerated in the villages – apparently without the handlers being bitten. They are then gently returned, unharmed, to their hiding places.

Top right: Primulas of many colours, such as the pink *Primula gracilipes* (above) and the yellow *Primula aureata* (below) brighten the upper slopes.

Right: Orchids in great profusion also grow in the lower forests; the beautiful *Dendrobium aphyllum* is a typical example.

58

Far left: The great forests of Himalayan Hemlock, *Tsuga dumosa*, and various firs and pines which once covered the lower slopes of the Nepalese Himalayas are rapidly disappearing because of the country's dependence on wood for fuel and building.

Top and above left: No flowers of the Himalayas can be more spectacular, nor grow in greater variety and profusion, than the rhododendron. The scarlet *Rhododendron arboreum* is one of several tree-rhododendrons that grow to a height of 15 metres.
Above right: At high altitudes, the scarlet Rhododendron is replaced by a pink variety of the same species, *R.a. cinnamomeum*.

Right: The Red Panda lives in the temperate forests of Nepal and Sikkim. Its bright reddish-orange fur and white face are conspicuous in daylight, but this animal usually spends most of the day sleeping, curled up on a high tree branch.

Above: The 'Slipper' orchid: *Paphiopedilum spicerianum.*

Top left and bottom right: The Red Lacewing butterfly *Cethosia biblis* with wings open and closed.

Top right: A yellow orchid: *Cymbidium elegans.*

Above: Mount Khangchendzonga from the mountain-top town of Darjeeling. Rising to 8197 metres, it guards the frontier between Sikkim and Nepal, where its peaks are called 'The Five Treasures of Eternal Snows'. Such views are possible only in the clear conditions that follow the months of the monsoon.

Right: A female Muntjak, or Barking Deer. Its name is derived from its distinctive dog-like barking call. It is fairly numerous in the thickly wooded hills up to an altitude of about 2500 metres. The males have short two-pronged antlers as well as short tusks.

Left: The Teesta River winds through the forested mountains of Sikkim. A rough road follows most of its course and provides access to some impressive scenery on the way to the capital, Gangtok.

Below: None of the small cats of India is more handsome than the little Leopard Cat, which is common in forests throughout the country. It continues to be much persecuted for its beautiful fur, despite being totally protected by law.

Above: The Hill Fox is the most likely of the three distinct races of the Red Fox to be seen in the Himalayan region. Like all foxes, it is a self-reliant and rather solitary animal, and eats a wide variety of food ranging from berries and offal to small birds and rodents. It is common around hill villages but seldom seen in the forest. The Indian Fox lives in the lowland plains.

Left: Oaks festooned with mosses and epiphytic orchids in Sikkim's Maenam Sanctuary.

63

Left: Forests are being destroyed for fuel or building throughout the Himalayan foothills, and scenes of devastation are commonplace. The top-soiled in felled areas is soon washed away by the monsoon rains, exposing villages to severe flooding.

Below left: The delicate flowers of the orchid *Pleione praecox* growing on a fallen oak in the Maenam Sanctuary.

Below right: The Goral is a goat-antelope of which two types, the grey and the brown, occur in the Himalayas at altitudes of 600–3700 metres. They have short, backward-curving horns and a distinctive, hissing alarm-cry.

Far left: The curious acorns of the evergreen oak *Lithocarpus pachyphylla* in the Maenam Sanctuary.

Centre left: Larvae of a Lymantriid moth in a communal nest.

Left: The Himalayan Palm Civet is distinguished from the various other civets of India by the absence of stripes or spots on its body, and by its long white whiskers. All the civets are useful as voracious hunters of rats, although this species feeds chiefly on fruit.

Overleaf: The peak of Mt. Kabur seen from Western Sikkim.

THE INDO-GANGETIC PLAIN
The Heartland of India

The great Indo-Gangetic Plain, forming the foredrop of the Himalayas, is probably the largest area of deposited alluvial soil in the world. No borehole has ever reached its base, thought to lie as deep as 13,000 metres. It consists of muds and sands washed down over the millennia from the Himalayan watershed, and even far below sea level it is still fine-grained. The seasonal rain-bearing winds of the monsoon, which sweep back and forth across the plain, make it one of the most productive, as well as one of the most densely populated regions on earth.

Its seemingly inexhaustible richness has tempted countless foreign invaders from less hospitable lands who laid waste so many of India's cities before being either repelled or quietly absorbed. This is the heartland of India and the chief source of its nourishment.

Three distinct river systems water the great plain. One rises from the western Himalayas as the Indus and its tributaries, reaching the Arabian Sea near Karachi in Pakistan. The second, which also rises in this region, turns immediately eastwards among the mountains, past Lhasa in Tibet, finally to flow southward through eastern Assam as the Brahmaputra, and on through Bangladesh to the sea. The third has many tributaries, all draining the southern slopes of the Himalayas and uniting to form the mighty Ganges, the holy river of India.

To the north of the plain, at the foot of the Himalayas, malaria once prevented development of the lowland terai, but with the temporary suppression of the disease the region was rapidly exploited. The hill farmers have swarmed down to cultivate the rich alluvial soil. The emerald green of paddyfields is now marching steadily forward and domestic cattle are replacing much of the wildlife for which the terai was once famous. Fortunately, HM King Mahendra and his successor HM King Birendra acted in time to save Nepal's Tigers, One-horned Rhinoceroses and Barasingha or Swamp Deer by creating the Royal Chitwan National Park and the Royal Karnali (renamed Royal Bardia and later upgraded to a national park) and Royal Sukhla Phanta Wildlife Reserves. Here substantial areas of the beautiful forests and grassy swamps of the terai are expertly managed and protected for the benefit of wildlife and the future generations of Nepalis.

To the far west lies the hot and arid region of the Indus plain, embracing Punjab, Sind, Rajasthan, Kutch and northern Gujarat. Even these vast areas were not always desert. Archaeological finds have revealed that there was once a flourishing civilization here in the Indus valley. Poor agricultural practices, deforestation and over-grazing eventually turned the region into an arid plain where water-dependent wildlife could not survive. Deforestation and desertification have continued on the desert fringe, and it has been estimated that the desert is extending in the north-west at the alarming rate of roughly eight kilometres every decade. Yet even the desert has attractions for the naturalist in its specially adapted vegetation and desert animals such as the famous Wild Asses in the Little Rann of Kutch in the south-west, or the large, and beautiful, but much endangered, Great Indian Bustards of Rajasthan.

To the east, benefiting from very high monsoon rainfall, lie the lush tropical, semi-evergreen forests of Assam, the Bangladesh Hill Tracts and the tribal areas of Burma. Both the Brahmaputra and the Ganges make their tortuous way to the Bay of Bengal through the labyrinth of the Sundarbans swamps. The name Sundarbans means beautiful forest and it is indeed a region of exceptional biotic richness. This is the largest mangrove forest in the world. The mean temperature here exceeds 28°C (80°F), reaching 43°C (109°F) in March. The annual rainfall is about 3.5 metres. The viscous, muddy ground into which one can sink above the knees is created entirely by river-borne silt trapped by the mangrove roots. These arch out from the trees into the mud, where regiments of bayonet-like spikes, the pneumatophore roots, are exposed at low tide to obtain the oxygen which the saline mud cannot provide.

One third of the Sundarbans is in India and heavily populated (except for a large Tiger Reserve), but there are relatively few humans in the Bangladesh two-thirds: only fishermen in their picturesque boats and honey-collectors and woodcutters in their canoes, who ply from Khulna down the long labyrinth of muddy channels. Tigers here are completely aquatic, swimming strongly from island to island. During my explorations I found their pug marks on an island 4.5 kilometres out in the Bay of Bengal. From the vantage point of a boat one can see Chital Deer, Wild Boar, Estuarine Crocodiles, Macaque Monkeys and several hundred species of birds. Even the shining mud along the creeks is full of life: bug-eyed little amphibian Mud Skippers row themselves up the banks on their dorsal fins, and colourful Fiddler Crabs urgently pirouette and wave their grotesquely big single claws like semaphores to attract females to their holes. There are some areas of mangrove on the west coast of India and at the mouth of the Indus in Pakistan, but nowhere in such magnificence or extent as in the 80,000 square kilometres of the Sundarbans delta.

The central plain is vast. Cities and tens of thousands of small villages are scattered across it, but lost in its huge scale. Here, 15 per cent of the world's population toil on the land. The great majority are poor, living patiently from one season to the next, trusting that the harvest will not fail and leave them destitute. Many are too poor to own a plot of land; they follow a nomadic share-cropping existence, moving from one district to another, to weed, or harvest, or plant at the behest of the rich landowners.

Most of the natural vegetation of the plain has been severely damaged by the constant search for fuel, which can be provided only by lopping or felling the fast disappearing trees, or by burning dried cowdung. Nevertheless, in this region are some of India's most renowned and valuable National Parks and Sanctuaries, which a far-sighted Government has succeeded in protecting from the human pressures beyond their boundaries. In such carefully preserved areas as Kanha, Corbett, Kaziranga and many others can still be seen the full magnificence of India's original vegetation and wildlife. Nowhere can a more beautiful tract of open Sal forest be seen than in the Kanha National Park. When one of its now numerous Tigers stalks majestically in daylight through the trees, the sight is unforgettable. Few places can compare with the splendour of Corbett National Park, set against the backdrop of the lovely Siwalik Hills, where wild Elephants still roam. To ride a well-trained Elephant through the marshes of Kaziranga National Park, among its many One-horned Rhinoceroses, wild Buffaloes and countless deer is a privilege beyond words.

The Clouded Leopard has abnormally long canines.

The Hoolock Gibbon is the only true ape found in India. It occurs in the hill forests of Assam and in the Bangladesh Hill Tracts, where it swings from tree to tree with amazing agility. This gibbon's extremely long arms and lack of a tail make its appearance unmistakable. The male is black, with conspicuous white eyebrows, while the female is pale brown. Gibbons advertise their presence long

before they can be seen with astonishingly loud *whoop-whoop* cries which can be heard for nearly a kilometre. Next to the deep-throated roar of a tiger, the duetted chorus of gibbons is probably the most romantic and thrilling sound to be heard anywhere. When a gibbon is calling, it inflates its throat like a balloon to produce a great volume of sound (second from right).

Above: A Buffalo cow guarding her twin calves among burned elephant grass, where they feed on the succulent young shoots.

A Pallas's Fishing Eagle in the Kaziranga National Park.

Left: Wild Buffaloes before a stand of elephant grass in Kaziranga National Park, in Assam, where there are still considerable numbers. Their massive horns, triangular in section, can have a span of more than two metres. Whereas domestic buffaloes are the epitome of docility, being led or ridden by children in the paddy fields, their wild relatives are extremely shy of humans and difficult to approach. They can be very aggressive, the bulls sometimes killing domestic bulls that show an interest in their cows. They have even been known to attack tigers which prey on the cows and calves, though they rarely succeed in driving them away.

After the Elephant, the One-horned Rhinoceros is the largest animal in the subcontinent. The biggest surviving population is in the Kaziranga National Park in Assam, where they can be approached quite closely by tourists riding well-trained elephants. Although the rhinos appear to be very tame, it is inadvisable to approach a cow with calf, the park wardens often have to fire a shot in the air in order to avoid being charged. Poachers everywhere kill rhinos for the high sums fetched by their horns, which are believed to have magical or medicinal properties. In 1995 there were at least 1948 and possibly as many as 2100 rhinos throughout India and Nepal.

Below: The Lesser Adjutant Stork is a useful scavenger with a fondness for carrion.

Right: Elephants feeding in the marsh beside a *jheel*.

Above: A few wild Elephants can be seen in the Kaziranga National Park, where they feed in the cane-breaks or bathe in the marshes. Although there are still 20,000–24,000 left in India, the population is declining because of the reduction of undisturbed forests. Unlike African Elephants, they avoid open country unless driven by hunger to seek food in cultivated areas, where they severely damage crops. The breaking up of the great forests has resulted in serious interference with their seasonal migrations, and has led to conflict with farmers. Special measures are now being taken in India to provide protected areas large enough for these splendid animals. Project Elephant was launched in 1991 as the Indian National Elephant Conservation and Management Strategy. Modelled on Project Tiger, it aims to ensure the future survival of larger elephant populations and link fragmented habitats via protected corridors.

Left: A Crested Serpent Eagle
with a snake it has just caught.

Below: A group of Spot-billed Pelicans perch in a flowering Silk-cotton.

Left: Male and female (far left) Hog Deer grazing in burned elephant grass in the Kaziranga National Park. The name is derived from their habit of scuttling through the undergrowth with their heads held low, like Wild Boar. Although Tigers and Leopards find them easy prey, they remain plentiful in the few remaining tracts of floodplain grassland.

Above: Herds of Barasingha, or Swamp Deer, graze in the extensive marshes of the Kaziranga National Park. This group is made up only of hinds or immature males, the stags living in bachelor herds outside the rutting season. There are three races of Barasingha, and these are identified by the shape of their hooves. Those in Kaziranga in Assam belong to the *ranjitsinhi* race, which have large, splayed hooves suited to soft ground. Further west, in the Dudwa National Park in Uttar Pradesh State and in Nepal, is the slightly different *duvaeceli* race and in the Kanha National Park in Madhya Pradesh is the *branderi* race, which has neat, small hooves well suited to the hard ground of that region.

Overleaf: A frosty morning in a forested valley in Meghalaya, between Shillong and Cherrapunji. The trees are *Pinus khasya*.

Right: The Sangai, or Manipur Brow-antlered Deer is among the world's most endangered deer, now restricted to a single population of 100–150 in the *phumdi* (floating swamps) of Keibul Lamjao National Park in Manipur, India. This stag is following a hind across the boggy ground. Even this habitat is today gravely imperilled by wetland reclamation for agriculture, and fish farming.

Below: The coarse dark coat and long brow-tines are typical of the male Sangai. These deer live in small herds, hiding by day and emerging to feed at dusk and in the early morning.

Above: The semi-aquatic habitat of the Sangai is best approached by boat along a channel cut through the swamp.

Right: White-winged Wood Ducks are now extremely rare, but a few still exist in sheltered pools in the evergreen rain-forests of Assam and in the Chittagong Hill Tracts. A strategy to conserve the species is being developed by the Wildfowl and Wetlands Trust in England.

Left: A Sangai fawn.

Left: The shy Serow is a goat-antelope which lives a fairly solitary existence in the rocky, wooded gorges of the Himalayas and in the Mishmi Hills in Assam. Its short, cylindrical horns grow from pedicles just above the eyes.

Below left: Sheer cliffs with waterfalls are typical of the rugged scenery of the Cherrapunji escarpment near Shillong. The deep forested gorges (below right) provide secure refuge for many forms of wildlife.

Above: The Slow Loris belongs to the Loris family, and is found in the forests of north-east India and in the Hill Tracts of Bangladesh. This gentle, slow-moving little creature – only 35 cm long – feeds mainly on insects. It sometimes feeds upside-down, hanging by its hind feet and holding food in its hands. The Slow Loris also drinks upside-down from water trapped in the hollow of a branch. It is often seen as a pet in villages.

Left and far left: The elusive Binturong, often called the Bear Cat, belongs to the Civet family. It has dense, grizzled fur and long white whiskers, and spends most of its time in the trees, climbing rather slowly with the aid of its long, bushy, prehensile tail. Like all the civets, it is omnivorous, feeding chiefly on fruit, small birds and insects. Its range is from Nepal and Assam eastwards into Myanmar (Burma) and peninsular Malaysia.

Among India's many species of monkeys, none is more beautiful than the Golden Leaf Monkey, shown here in Bhutan's Royal Manas National Park. With its silky, pale gold fur and exceptionally long tail, it never fails to evoke exclamations of admiration from anyone fortunate enough to see one.

Above: An Elephant in the Manas Forest takes a dust bath, a habit in which elephants delight in the absence of water. The Asian species is easily distinguished from the African by its smaller ears and more rounded back. Unlike the African elephant, it is an animal of the dense humid forests – where there are plenty of bamboo thickets in which to shelter. It also occurs in hilly or even mountainous regions, emerging at dusk to feed in the valleys. In Sikkim it has even been recorded above the snow line at 3660 metres. The cows have only rudimentary tusks, while those of the bulls rarely match the length of the African species.

Right: The Great Indian Hornbill is the largest of the half-dozen Indian species. It is easily distinguished by its huge bill (with a yellow casque) and its broad black and white wings, which make a distinctive noise – like those of a Mute Swan – in flight. Like all the hornbills, it is now suffering from the loss of old forest trees, with large cavities in which to nest.

Above: An Elephant in the Manas Forest.

Centre left: The fallen flower of a Silk Cotton Tree, *Bombax ceiba*.

Left: A hoary-bellied Himalayan Squirrel in the hill forests of Manas.

Above and top: The large and handsome Malayan Giant Squirrel can be seen in Nepal, Bhutan and Assam. It is recognized by its almost black upper parts and bright orange-buff underparts. When alarmed by a predator, such as a Leopard, it gives a very loud, rattling cry which can be heard for a great distance.

Left: The broad Manas River divides India from the Kingdom of Bhutan. By good co-operative planning, the Indian Manas Tiger Reserve and Bhutan Royal Manas National Park now adjoin on either side of the river. The two protected areas cover a combined area of 1,366 square kilometres and constitute one of the least despoiled areas of continuous primary forest, which is exceptionally rich in rare species of animals and plants. Animal photography in such dense forest is difficult, partly because the ground is usually carpeted with dry fallen leaves which crackle underfoot and alarm the animals.

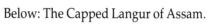

Left: The delicate white flowers of a species of *Apolynaceae*.

Below left: The Muntjak or Barking Deer, whose dog-like barking call is easily imitated. Manas Forest.

Below: The Capped Langur of Assam.

Above and right: The large Water Monitor is one of the many strange amphibious creatures that live in the Sundarbans. It prowls the labyrinth of muddy channels, digging up the eggs of turtles and crocodiles and killing rodents and nesting birds.

Left: The largest area of mangrove swamp in the world is in the Sundarbans, at the mouth of the Ganges, Meghna and Brahmaputra rivers. The dominant tree species is the Sundri, *Heritiera fomes*, with dense clumps of various palms such as *Phoenix paludosa* (foreground) – favourite tiger habitat. A third of the Sundarbans lies in India, with the remaining two-thirds in Bangladesh.

Below right: To land here is to sink up to the thighs in the glutinous mud and to stumble along the intricately interwoven arched roots of the mangroves. These roots trap the silt from the water and gradually build up islands. To obtain oxygen, which the saline mud cannot provide, the trees grow regiments of bayonet-like spikes from their roots, which at low tide are exposed to the air.

Above: Everywhere are thousands of colourful Fiddler Crabs, named after their habit of waving a grotesquely large claw to attract females to their holes.

Centre top: The bug-eyed little Mud Skipper is an amphibious fish which 'rows' itself up the banks on its dorsal fins to feed among the mangrove roots.

Right: At Bhitar Kanika Sanctuary, on the Orissa coast, Salt-water, or Estuarine, Crocodiles can be seen basking on the banks of the Mahanadi River. At one time they were very nearly exterminated by skin traders, but here and elsewhere there are now special breeding and research centres, from where the species is being reintroduced to the wild.

Below: A handsome Black Carpenter Bee, *Xylocopa sp.*, feeding on a *Crotolaria* flower.

Bottom: *Borassus* and *Phoenix* palms against the sunset.

Above: The Pangolin, or Scaly Anteater, is a familiar animal throughout India. It feeds on termites or ants, which are dug out with powerful claws. During daylight, the Pangolin is usually hidden in a deep burrow, coming out to feed in the evenings. A ponderous walker, this animal supports most of its weight on very long, in-turned front claws. When surprised, it rolls itself up into an impregnable ball.

Left: There are about 20 species of mangroves in the Sundarbans and along the Orissa coast, the most typical being those with long arched roots, like the *Bruguiera gymnorhiza* shown here.

Left: Long-billed Vultures were once common in India, but in recent years have been decimated by feeding off diclofenac-medicated carcasses (see page 151). Vultures roam the skies at very high altitudes, looking for carrion and watching each other. The moment one bird drops, the others immediately follow it down to the carcass, so that scores may assemble in a matter of minutes.

Below: A Blue Tiger Butterfly, *Tirumala limniace* – one of the milkweed group.

Bottom: The Chilka Lake Sanctuary in Orissa.

Above and left: The White Tigers of Rewa are world famous. They are neither albinos (which would have pink eyes) nor a separate species, but are what scientists call 'recessive mutants'. In 1951 a white cub was trapped in the Rewa forest and kept as a pet by the local Maharajah, who mated it to a normal captive tigress. She produced three normal litters. One of her cubs was later mated with the white sire, producing a litter of white cubs which were the ancestors of others now in many zoos.

Overleaf: A Tiger in Kanha National Park. The Tiger is India's magnificent 'national animal' and is the subject of India's most famous conservation effort.

Left and bottom: The Kanha National Park in Madhya Pradesh is noted for its open Sal forests, which the Chital, or Spotted Deer, particularly favours. It is generally regarded as the most beautiful of the world's many deer species, and is common in the forest glades of many of India's sanctuaries. The stag's antlers have only three long tines, and their coats are sometimes almost black. The antlers are dropped at varying times in different localities, although pairing is usually in the winter. Fawns may be seen in all seasons.

Below: A Little Green Bee-eater, one of a number of colourful species of this family in India.

Above left: A mixed flock of Green Pigeons, Plum-headed Parakeets and Rose-ringed Parakeets.

Far left: Dholes, or Wild Dogs, in the Kanha National Park. They hunt in packs with ruthless efficiency, preying mainly on deer. Even tigers avoid them.

Left: Jackals scavenge around all villages, but are now much less numerous than they used to be.

Above: Although Gaur, or Indian Bison, look so powerful (a bull weighs nearly one ton), they are timid and retiring creatures. Family groups spend most of the day hidden in the dense hill forests, descending to the grassy valleys to feed at dusk and dawn. Once fairly widely distributed in the hilly regions, it is now very localized. Gaur can be seen in such protected areas as Chitwan in Nepal and Bandipur and Mudumalai in the Western Ghats in southern India, as well as Kanha and the forests of central India.

Above, top and right: There are some fine herds of the *branderi* race of Barasingha in the Kanha National Park, where they are a favoured prey species of Tigers. The stags have dark coats and well-branched antlers. When fully grown, they can weigh up to 180 kg, with heavy manes and antlers measuring up to 75 cm. Barasingha are strongly gregarious. If alarmed, they will dash off with a loud chorus of distinctive baying. The Kanha population, the last in central India and which had declined to less than 66 by the mid-1960s, now numbers 450–550. It is gratifying to note that the Baiga and Gond tribal people of the regions, who used to be skilled hunters of the Swamp Deer, now take obvious pride in protecting the wildlife in this superb national park. There is talk of introducing the species to Satpura Tiger Reserve.

Below left: Mynah birds feed off parasites on a Barasingha hind.

Below right: The colourful Indian Roller is common throughout the country.

The Bandhavgarh National Park in Madhya Pradesh State has a wide range of wildlife species, including Tigers and some rare birds. It is a scenically remarkable area, with high rocky outcrops and cliffs.

Right: A pair of Black Ibises.

Below: A Dusky Eagle Owl, with its 'horns' depressed.

Below right: This rocky cliff is typical of the Park's terrain, which is crowned with an ancient fortress and temple ruins.

Above: The Crested Serpent Eagle is fairly common in the wooded parts of the northern half of India. It is replaced to the south of the Gangetic Plain by a slightly smaller race, the Lesser Crested Eagle. As its name implies, it feeds on snakes, lizards and frogs, but also takes crabs, eels and small birds. It often soars to a great height, when it is readily identified by its distinctive high whistling cry.

Left: When suspicious, and during courtship, the Crested Serpent Eagle erects its fan-shaped crest.

In 1900 there were perhaps 40,000 Tigers in India.
By 1972 a census showed that only 1,827 survived.
Loss of forest habitat was a major factor in this
catastrophic decline, combined with increasingly
excessive hunting. It was clear that unless an
enormous effort could be made to save them,
Tigers would be extinct within 20 years. With the
help of a world-wide campaign organized by the
World Wide Fund for Nature, the Indian
Government launched 'Project Tiger' in 1973.
This has resulted in a complete ban on hunting and
the creation of 23 fully protected Tiger reserves
which cover over 30,000 square kilometres and
contain about 1,300 tigers, approximately one-third
of India's population of 3,750. Thanks to skilful
management of the vegetation and water resources,
not only have the initial prospects of Tigers and
their prey species improved but all wildlife has
benefited.

Above and right: Tiger cubs with their mother.

Top right: A tree regularly used by a Tiger for
sharpening its claws.

The Royal Chitwan National Park is expertly managed, and has been the scene of a number of important wildlife research projects in which Nepalese, British and American scientists have shared the work. The first studies of the territorial behaviour of Tigers by means of radio telemetry were conducted there, the Tigers being fitted with collars bearing miniature radio transmitters. This research was under the auspices of the Nepalese Government, the Smithsonian Institution and the World Wide Fund for Nature, and today there is close co-operation between Nepalese and Indian tiger experts. Tourists from the 'Tiger Tops Lodge' can watch One-horned Rhinoceroses and Sloth Bears and several species of deer feeding in the marshes. There are also well-hidden hides from which Tigers and Leopards can be seen at night. In the rivers there are both Mugger Crocodiles and Gharials as well as Gangetic Dolphins. Some 489 species of birds have been recorded in the Park.

Right: The banks of the Rapti River in the Royal Chitwan National Park in Nepal provide an admirable vantage point for the panorama of changing colours on the distant Himalayas, photographed late on a November day. The snowy peaks are over 200 km away, and such views are possible only in the clear air that follows the monsoon.

Top left: There are many marshy pools and streams in the Royal Chitwan National Park where Tigers bathe and Rhinoceroses wallow.

Above: A male Iora at its nest, woven of fine grasses and spiders' webs.

Right: A parasitic 'left-handed' Strangler Fig squeezing the life out of the host tree in its struggle to reach the sunlight.

Opposite: The presence of Rhinoceroses is easily detected by the big heaps of dung which serve to provide information on the whereabouts and reproductive condition of individuals. The rhino's habit of backing up to the heap to add a new quota is well known to poachers, who traditionally dig camouflaged pit traps along the established approach tracks. Strangely enough, a few old rhinos are known to have lost their aggressive spirit, staying near villages and even allowing children to ride on them. However, such behaviour is exceptional.

Below: The Green Pit Viper occurs in the Nepalese *terai*. Like the Cobra and other venomous species, it helps to control the huge rat population.

Bottom left: The butterfly, *Papilio polytes*.

Bottom right: The so-called 'bloodsucker' or Garden Lizard, *Calotes versicolor*.

Right: The Royal Chitwan National Park affords an opportunity to see fully adult Gharials; a captive breeding centre for them has been established on the Rapti River in the Park. Males can grow up to 7 metres long, and have large, bulbous tips to their upper jaws. In spite of their size and fierce appearance, they are harmless fish-eaters. Those shown below are only two years old.

Right and below: The Dudwa National Park, on the border between India and Nepal, is one of the strongholds of the Barasingha, or Swamp Deer, with a particularly fine herd of the *duvauceli* race. The population has declined from 1200–1500 in 1976 to some 700 by 1993, primarily due to hunting – part of the population spends over half of the year outside the park, where Barasingha are particularly prone to being poached. Dudwa is also the home of a considerable number of Tigers and Leopards, and is among the latest of India's Tiger reserves to be established under Project Tiger. It was here that the famous naturalist, Billy Arjan Singh, reared several orphaned Tiger and Leopard cubs and successfully returned them to the wild, a feat never achieved before. He was largely instrumental in the creation of the park, which has some tracts of very beautiful forest and extensive grassy *maidans* where the deer feed.

Below: The Red Jungle Fowl, the progenitor of the domestic chicken.

Left and centre: Peafowl are numerous in the Dudwa National Park. The magnificent fan is displayed during the male's courtship dance, which occurs during the later part of the dry season.

Far left: A walk in the Dudwa National Park at dawn reveals the full beauty of the forest as the sun illuminates its rich colours.

Left: The red tree along this forest path is a Kusum, or *Schleichera oleosa*. The bright colour is provided by the tree's young leaves.

Far left: The Corbett National Park at dawn. The Park, in Uttar Pradesh, was named after the renowned hunter-naturalist, Jim Corbett, who was the first to publicize the threats to the survival of the Tiger in the 1940s. The park is scenically magnificent, set against the backdrop of the Siwalik Hills, with the Ramganga River winding through it. The recent damming of the river just downstrean of this point deprived the wild elephants of their favourite feeding area and interrupted their long-established seasonal route. However, the park remains one of the most attractive in India, and is still rich in wildlife.

Left: A Plum-headed Parakeet eating a wild fig.

Below left: A White-throated Kingfisher.

Below: A Large-tailed Nightjar in the Corbett National Park.

Right: A pair of the attractive little Collared Scops Owls, whose quiet *'wheet . . . wheet'* cry can be monotonous at night. The Indian sub-continent has nearly 50 different species and regional sub-species of owl.

Far left: Spoonbills can be seen in many wetland areas in India, Nepal and Bangladesh. In breeding plumage, with long, drooping crests and bright orange feathers at the base of the neck, they are very handsome birds. Part of the Indian population is migratory. Spoonbills breed in mixed colonies, with various storks, ibises and herons as close neighbours.

Left and below: A Spoonbill carries a large twig to add to its nest.

Above and right: A courtship ritual of the Rose-ringed Parakeet. This bright green species is common in all city parks and gardens, its noisy flocks dashing around the roof-tops. Although handsome, it can ravage cereal and fruit crops. Marauding flocks ignore the slings and catapults of the bird-scarers posted on their *machans* around the fields. These birds nest under roof-tiles and in cavities in wayside trees, not only in towns, but also in forested and even arid regions. These pictures show a courting pair. Courtships involve mutual preening, the passing of food to the female and a curious clawing of the air by the male followed by wild chases in flight.

Below: Northern Pintails in Keoladeo National Park.

Below centre: Red-crested Pochard feeding.

Bottom: A Five-striped Ground Squirrel.

Above: Black-headed Ibises, of which hundreds nest
in congested colonies.

Keoladeo National Park, often referred to as Bharatpur, provides
one of the greatest wildlife spectacles in India. Its many ponds,
tree-lined *bunds* and lush meadows are literally crowded with a
vast congregation of birds of many kinds. It is also an important
centre for bird-ringing and ornithological research, much of
which is organized by the Bombay Natural History Society, and
for public education by the Indian branch of the World Wide
Fund for Nature.

Right: Black-headed Ibis chicks can barely move in their
overcrowded nest.

Left: A White-backed Vulture with chick at its huge nest. This
species is now extinct in the park.

Right: Painted Storks also nest by the hundred in the Keoladeo National Park.

Above: The most important visitors to Keoladeo are the ultra-rare Siberian Cranes, a pair of which is shown here. Every year a flock normally arrives from the USSR to winter in the safety of the park, but the number has been steadily declining from nearly 200 in 1965 to 17 in the winter of 1989/90 and just four in 1996. None were observed in the park during the winters of 1993/94 and 1994/95. This population, which breeds in the Kunovat region of western Siberia, is critically endangered, many cranes never completing their migration through Pakistan and Afghanistan where they are hunted. Ornithologists gather at Keoladeo every year to watch their fascinating courtship 'dancing'.

Right: A Nilgai cow and Cattle Egret in the Keoladeo marshes.

Left: Young Intermediate Egrets at their nest.

Below: A Darter drying its wings after swimming beneath the water in one of the ponds.

Bottom: Even at dusk and before sunrise, the ponds are alive with birds.

Right: The Openbill Stork is the most numerous of India's various storks. Its curiously shaped bill is specially adapted to slicing open the shells of the snails and other crustaceans on which it feeds. The Openbill Stork has a remarkable display flight, descending vertically, twisting and turning while 'pedalling' its long legs vigorously.

Below: A huge flight of Greylag Geese take off from the Keoladeo marshes.

Left: An Asian Openbill.

Above: A Black-necked Stork. This handsome but rather solitary bird with coral-red legs has the black areas of its plumage glossed with purple, blue and bronze, making it one of the most attractive of the storks.

Left: The Tawny Eagle is a common species throughout India. It is rather lethargic, feeding mainly on carrion or forcing other raptors to relinquish their prey.

Far left and below left: Birds are so numerous at Keoladeo that there is a shortage of nesting sites. Colonial species such as Painted Storks nest so closely together in the acacias that their nests merge, leading to continuous squabbling and much stealing of twigs.

Left: A Painted Stork in flight.

Below: Often a single tree houses several different species. Two pairs of Spoonbills have built nests directly beneath those in which young Painted Storks are standing. A Grey Heron and a Darter fish from the same tree.

Right: The Nilgai, or Blue Bull, with a Tree Pie riding on its back in Rajasthan's Sariska Sanctuary. The Nilgai is something of a curiosity: it has none of the grace of the antelopes to which it is related. Instead, it is ungainly, with too small a head and sloping haunches. Its rudimentary horns are bent forward and it runs awkwardly, like a Giraffe, with its head held high. Because of its somewhat cow-like appearance, it is protected by Hindus, and sportsmen disdain shooting it.

Right centre: A female Nilgai with two young. The females are more cow-like than the males.

Below: A group of Red-vented Bulbuls hesitantly slake their thirst.

Below right: A Laughing Dove drinks at a water hole.

Below: The largest crane in India is the crimson-headed Sarus. When standing erect it is as tall as a man. It is noted for its loud trumpeting calls and elaborate courtship, which involves much leaping, bowing and prancing. In India it is venerated as a symbol of fidelity and family unity because it pairs for life.

Below left: A herd of Nilgai sheltering from the sun under *Phoenix dactalifera* palms in the Sariska Sanctuary.

Below right: The flower of *Capparis decidua*.

133

Rhesus Macaque monkeys in the Sariska Sanctuary. These familiar animals are seen throughout the northern half of India, and are never molested by humans. They are easily distinguished from other species by their orange-red bottoms. Large numbers occur in towns and villages, railway stations and temples, where they beg for food or steal it from wayside stalls. In the wild they prefer roadsides and the edges of forests, and spend more time on the ground than most other monkey species. Those in the Himalayan region have thicker fur, and have been seen at altitudes of up to 3800 metres in Nepal. In the hotter regions they dive and swim strongly in canals and water tanks. Great numbers were once exported to the United States and Europe – particularly from Bangladesh – for medical research purposes. However, exports are now controlled.

135

Right and far right: 'The Peacock is the glory of God,' says an early Sanskrit document. These beautiful birds are numerous in India and Pakistan. They were chosen as the 'national bird of India', and they certainly provide a splendid spectacle as they fly about in the Himalayan foothills, or over wildlife reserves. The long, eyed feathers of the males' trains are carefully collected and sold in the village markets for making fans or temple decorations.

Below: A Sambar hind at a water hole in Sariska.

Bottom centre: *Sterculia* trees in flower.

Above: Pythons are India's largest snakes, some growing to a length of seven metres and capable of crushing prey up to the size of a small deer in their powerful coils.

Right: Wild Boar, the same species as is found in Europe, cause great losses to Indian farmers, and are almost impossible to keep away from crops. They are a common prey of Tigers, and in areas where these large predators have disappeared, farmers soon learn – largely through the dramatic increase in the Boar population – how crucial a role was played by the Tigers.

Above and right: Chital Deer at a waterhole in the Sariska Sanctuary. The very long antlers of a full-grown stag are illustrated in the picture on the right. These beautiful deer usually move about in herds of up to 30, but occasionally build up to 100 or more, with several stags in attendance. Although preyed upon constantly by Tigers, Leopards and Dholes, they breed freely and their numbers in protected areas remain high and in some cases may be increasing.

Top right: Langurs drinking.

Right: A pair of Chinkara Gazelles in the Ranthambore National Park in Rajasthan. Small numbers of these gazelles still inhabit the dry areas of north-western India and parts of the Deccan plateau. They are slender and extremely agile animals, capable of short bursts of very high speed when chased by a predator. They can go for long periods without water, obtaining all they need from the dry desert vegetation.

Below: The dragonfly *Brachythemis contaminata*.

Above: A White-necked Stork, a Peacock and several vultures with a herd of Chital Deer in the Ranthambore National Park. Such mixed gatherings are frequent at water-holes on the edges of forests – particularly at dawn and dusk, when the big cats lie in wait in the undergrowth to pick off the unwary coming to drink.

Left: A large monitor lizard, the Common Indian Monitor *Varanus bengalensis*, investigates a hollow tree in the park.

Far left: A Pond Heron, or Paddy-bird, on the lily *Nymphoides indica*. Paddy-birds are almost as common as Cattle Egrets around rice fields. When they fly, their appearance is transformed by their snow-white wings.

141

Above left: The inquisitive Jungle Babbler is typical of the many species of this family of birds in India, some of which are fine songsters. It is noisy and very active, moving about in the undergrowth in small, busy groups.

Top, above and far right: Ranthambore has a large population of graceful black-faced Langur monkeys in the forested areas. They live in large troops and feed on flowers, fruit and leaves.

Right: The bole of a Banyan tree, a member of the ubiquitous fig family, showing the mass of roots which descend from its branches, enabling it to spread over a great area. One tree still growing in the Botanic Gardens in Calcutta, and known to have been planted as a seed in 1782, has a circumference of over 420 metres.

Right: Sambar hinds, each with a Black Drongo on its back hawking the insects disturbed by the deer.

Below: Sambar spend much of their time in or near water, taking mud-baths.

Bottom: Mature Sambar stags with the shaggy mane and heavy antlers characteristic of the species.

Above: The butterfly *Precis hierta*.

Left: The commensal relationship between birds and deer is again illustrated by this Sambar hind in Ranthambore, which is closely followed by a Great White Egret and a Grey Heron. The birds snap up insects and frogs disturbed by the hind's progress throught the marsh. Even Rhinoceroses are followed in this manner.

Left: Leopards have survived better in India than Tigers because they are more adaptable to changing conditions. The reduction of forests has driven many of them to living near villages, where they prey on domestic animals such as goats, donkeys and poultry. There are stories of Leopards boldly snatching pet dogs from verandahs while the owners sit nearby. Being expert tree climbers, they kill many monkeys, and will carry a deer or a Wild Boar up into the branches to eat it at leisure. Like Tigers, their role in the ecology of the forest is a positive one because they cull the weak or sickly animals and help to control the population of those which are too numerous.

Above: A Common Tiger butterfly, *Danaus genutia*.

Top left: A Red-headed Vulture.

Top right: A Tigress in the Ranthambore National Park.

Left: A Jungle Cat in the Ranthambore National Park.

Tal Chapar Sanctuary in Rajasthan was specially set up to protect one of the most striking and agile of India's animals, the Blackbuck. Excessive hunting very nearly exterminated this animal but fortunately some of the herds kept by the Maharajahs enabled the species to survive. It is now strictly protected in places such as Tal Chapar, Dharwa and Guda near Jodhpur, where the local Bishnoi people have traditionally protected it. There are other areas specially protected for Blackbuck, notably Velavadar National Park in Gujarat and Ranebennur Sanctuary in Karnataka.

Right: Blackbuck females with a young male and two mature males. Tal Chapar.

In Pakistan, Blackbuck were virtually exterminated by the 1950s, but with the initial help of the World Wide Fund for Nature they are being restored to the Lal Suhanra National Park. The reintroduction programme began in 1970 with 10 animals from a Texas ranch, descendants of Blackbuck sent to Texas in 1940. In the early 1980s further stocks were obtained from zoos in Copenhagen and New South Wales.

Far left and above: Blackbuck are very elegant animals, the males having long spiral horns and handsome, almost black-and-white coats. During the rut they adopt a curious mincing gait, with their heads held almost vertically, while maintaining a long series of grunting notes. They fight vigorously for control of the females.

Left: When alarmed, Blackbuck take off in a series of high leaps, like African Impalas, before breaking into a swift gallop. In the old days, the Maharajahs used to enjoy the sport of having them hunted by Cheetahs, but these animals are now extinct in India.

Right: Half a dozen species of vulture are found in India. This group, photographed after a feast, consists of Long-billed, White-backed and King Vultures.

Above: The much smaller Egyptian Vulture, two of which also appear at the edge of the group far left.

Far left and top: It took these birds some twenty minutes to pick the body of a dead cow to bare bones. The hungry village pie-dog joined the crowd to take advantage of a hasty meal.

Left: After feasting on this carcass, the vultures were unable to fly. Instead, they stood around digesting their meal before taking off like over-laden aircraft. Unfortunately, the use of diclofenac, an anti-inflammatory drug used for cattle, has had a devastating impact on India's vultures, reducing the population of some species by up to 90 per cent.

Right and far right: Bar-headed Geese are migrants to India, crossing the Himalayas from central Asia to reach their winter feeding grounds in reserves such as the Dharwa Lake and Keoladeo.

Bottom right: A flock of beautiful Demoiselle Cranes, which are also migratory. They suffer considerable losses from hunters who sling weighted cords into their passing flocks in Afghanistan and Pakistan.

Below: the fruit of the shrub *Capparis decidua*.

Above: A Demoiselle Crane with a broken wing, probably caused by flying into an overhead power line.

Right: The Desert National Park in the great Thar Desert in Rajasthan is a hostile region with extremely high temperatures. However, it is scenically beautiful where the prevailing winds pile up the sand into Sahara-like dunes. Rain may not fall for a year or more, yet in this harsh environment wildlife still thrives, each species in an elaborate ecosystem which has evolved to take advantage of the available resources. In the absence of rain, dew is drunk from the tips of the sparse grasses, and plants find moisture by thrusting their roots metres-deep into the ground. Many plants are highly specialized. Even mushrooms grow where daytime temperatures can exceed 45°C. A host of strange beetles, lizards, skinks and snakes live on or beneath the surface of the sand. Hardy Desert Hares and Gerbils find shelter in the brittle vegetation, where they are preyed upon by Jackals, Desert Foxes, Desert Cats and a host of birds of prey.

Far right: The wild melon *Citrullus colocynthis*. When ripe, the round fruit is bowled far across the desert by the wind, thus enabling it to disperse its seed.

Right: A *tenebrionid* beetle leaves its track across the desert sand.

Below: Three of the now extremely rare Great Indian Bustards. These large and stately birds are greatly endangered by the steady encroachment of cultivation into the undisturbed grasslands which are their habitat. Serious losses have also been caused by poachers who shoot them from jeeps or from slow-moving bullock carts, to which the bustards pay little attention. The bustards are strictly protected in the Desert National Park and some other protected areas, such as the Bustard Sanctuaries at Ghatigaon in Madhya Pradesh and the Naliya grasslands in Kutch, but their numbers are still critically small. They used to be plentiful as far south as the plains of the Deccan, where (in 1829) a sportsman once boasted that he had shot 961 of them. Most bustards occur in Rajasthan and are occasionally also found in Gujarat, Maharastra, Karnataka and Andra Pradesh. Their large eggs, laid on bare ground, are constantly preyed upon by House Crows and Civets. They have an elaborate courtship, the males leaping into the air, rapidly fanning their tails over their backs and inflating their throat-pouches until they hang down between their legs like wobbling balloons.

Top: Winter at the edge of the Thar Desert, with a Laggar Falcon at its roost on a thorn-tree.

Far right: A desert plant, *Calotropis procera*.

Right: Flowering clumps of the desert grass *Eragrostris plumosa*.

157

Above: The Kumbhalgarh Sanctuary is in a part of
Rajasthan where the scenery changes dramatically.
The desert here gives way to huge outcrops of
eroded basaltic or granitic rocks and deep gorges.

Top right: *Euphorbia* bushes and (in winter) a profusion
of Cassia spread a colourful canopy across the dry plain.

Middle: The yellow *Cassia auriculata*.

Above: In this area, desert species make way for moisture-loving creatures such as this stout Ground Boa.

Right: As soon as trees begin to appear, the familiar Grey Langurs can be heard chattering – and the transition from desert to almost temperate forest is complete.

Below: Perhaps the bleakest, dustiest and hottest region in India is the Great Rann of Kutch. It stretches for hundreds of square kilometres in the State of Gujarat, from the frontier with Pakistan's Sind desert, southward to the Little Rann and the Gulf of Kutch. It is a desolate area of unrelieved, sun-baked saline clay desert, shimmering with the images of a perpetual mirage.

Above and right: The Little Rann is the last refuge of the Indian Wild Ass, an exceptionally hardy animal which contrives to live and even breed in this harsh environment, feeding on the withered grass which grows in the depressions. There were once many thousands of Wild Asses roaming the dry plains of India, but their numbers steadily declined, mainly because of diseases, to 362 in 1967. Conservation measures proved so successful that by 1983 the population had increased to almost 2000 individuals. They are no longer hunted, although poachers kill a few and soldiers (this is a sensitive frontier region) sometimes harass them by chasing them in jeeps.

Left: A pair of Pied Kingfishers.

Below left: A profusion of white flowers against a rich blue sky.

Below: *Cassia fistula*.

Top left: The Gir National Park in Gujarat, now one of the most important in India, was once the property of the Nawabs of Junagadh. Over-run by land-hungry villagers after the Partition of India, the forest was the last refuge of the Asiatic Lion, of which there were still about 300 in 1955. With the loss of vegetation, the deer on which the Lions fed soon disappeared, and they began to starve. By 1968, only 177 survived. The Gujarat State then turned the forest into a protected area and re-settled the villagers elsewhere. The Lions had sufficient prey, with the result that by 1990 their numbers had increased to an estimated 221 adults, with an additional 30–40 lions believed to live in the surrounding agricultural land. By 2006 the population had grown further to over 330.

Far left: The colouring of these Painted Sandgrouse hens merges with the forest floor to provide a fine camouflage.

Left: The more brightly coloured Painted Sandgrouse cock, whose plumage earns the species its name.

The Gir Lions are the Asiatic, forest-loving relatives of the African Lion. Their range once extended from Greece to central India, but those in the Gir are the last survivors – of which India is rightly proud. The National Park is one of the best-managed in the country, and provides good facilities for visitors to see these unique animals in their forest habitat.

Overleaf: A fine pride of Lions in the Gir National Park.

THE DECCAN
The Southern Tableland of India

In the days of conquest, before roads and railways physically unified India, the great triangular southern peninsula was almost a different world, divided from the Indo-Gangetic plain, from east to west, by the scattered ranges of the Vindhya Mountains. These are neither very high nor quite continuous, but in the early days were linked in the valleys by hostile jungle which discouraged penetration. Today the barrier effect is less evident, but geographically the difference between north and south of the Vindhyas remains self-evident.

Instead of the endless flat plain, little above sea level, the Deccan peninsula is based on raised granitic rock. In the north-west, in what geologists call the Deccan trap, are extensive outflows of ancient basaltic lava, capped more recently with laterite. Down either side of the peninsula, like sea-walls, run the long ranges of the Western and Eastern Ghats. Their average elevations are respectively about 1000 and 500 metres, with here and there peaks rising to twice or three times as high. They merge at the southern tip of the triangle to form the plateau of the beautiful Nilgiri Hills, with the Dodabetta peak triumphantly marking the junction.

The Western Ghats rise abruptly from a narrow coastal plain as an unbroken challenge to the south-west monsoon. The high rainfall on their seaward slopes produces a heavy cladding of luxurious rain forest. From their eastern flanks flow fast-running rivers, some of which, such as the Godavari, the Cauvery and the Krishna, traverse the whole tableland, winding through the minor inland mountains to drain by the valleys through the Eastern Ghats into the Bay of Bengal. The less spectacular Eastern Ghats do not hug the shore as closely, but are fragmented with a broader belt of coastal lowlands. They too are forested, but the vegetation is less lush than on their western counterparts. Here, in southern India, the high mountain slopes and forests of the Nilgiris have similar species to those of the Assam ranges -including a distinctive Tahr (wild goat) and a Langur monkey. Sal woodlands to the north give way to teak and semi-evergreen tropical forest in the south. Throughout the southern peninsula scenery is far more varied and dramatic than in the Indo-Gangetic Plain. The industrious people of southern India are also more varied than their northern neighbours and maintain many colourful traditions and religious festivals throughout the year.

The inland hill regions often enjoy a delightful climate and are of surpassing beauty. In the days of the British raj places such as Ootacamund were often preferred to Kashmir or Darjeeling as hot-weather retreats. Elegant houses with names such as 'Journey's End' or 'Rose Cottage' were built there, each with a traditional English garden, full of such favourites as Delphiniums and Marguerites, but now being reclaimed for more contemporary development.

Wildlife is abundant in the less accessible parts of the Deccan and many splendid Sanctuaries and National Parks have been established. Tigers and their prey species are thriving in the teak and bamboo forests. In the south they can be seen in the Bandipur National Park in Karnataka and in the tropical evergreen jungle of Periyar in Kerala. The rare and very striking Lion-tailed Macaque monkey has its last refuge in the rain forests of the Western Ghats, and some 6000 wild Elephants still roam the dense forests at the convergence of the Stages of Karnataka, Kerala and Tamil Nadu.

In the protected areas particular attention is now paid to maintaining freshwater pools and streams, most of which would normally run dry in the hot season. It is to them that wildlife must come to drink and bathe. An observation post near one of them is one of the best ways of seeing Tigers, Elephants and various deer during the summer months.

Crocodiles and several species of big sea turtles have received special protection at certain localities on the coasts of the peninsula and vast numbers of various wading birds abound near all of the picturesque fishing villages. Even around the great coastal cities, such as Bombay and Madras, a considerable variety of wildlife lives in parks and gardens. Throughout the region, peninsular India provides a breath-taking abundance of colour, variety and interest for the naturalist.

A coastal scene in Goa, on the west coast of India. This was once a Portuguese colony.

Right: A coastal forest of Toddy Palms, *Borassus flabellifer* near Madras.

Below: Vine snakes or Common Green Whip Snakes (*Ahaetulla nasuta*) with a Bronzeback Tree Snake, *Dendrelaphis sp*.

Bottom left: Fallen fruit of the Toddy Palm.

Bottom right: The Indian Chameleon (*Chamaeleo zeylanicus*).

Right: The Great White Egret is the largest of the four egret species in India. In the breeding season, the upper parts of its legs are flushed with orange and the skin at the base of its bill turns bright blue. Like the other egrets it erects the long scapular feathers on its back during courtship to form a delicate white cloak.

Above: A Cattle Egret in full breeding plumage.

Above left: Indian Flying Foxes roosting in a tree in the Sanctuary.

Left: A colony of Streak-throated Swallows at their bottle-shaped mud nests beside the Cauvery River in the Ranganthittu Sanctuary.

Far left: A Mugger, or Marsh Crocodile, basks on an exposed rock in the Cauvery River in the Ranganthittu Sanctuary, Karnataka State.

Left: Colonies of Night Herons nest at Ranganthittu.

Below: From left to right are a Little Egret, an Asian Openbill, an Intermediate Egret and a Cattle Egret. The Little Egret is clearly distinguished by its small size, fine black bill and black legs with yellow feet (which are here hidden in the mud); the Intermediate Egret has a yellow bill and black legs; the Cattle Egret has a much shorter, flesh-coloured bill and a distinctive, heavy jowl.

Overleaf: A drowned forest in the Kabbani River, Karnataka.

Top: Elephants bathing in a *jheel* in the Nagarahole National Park. This park, in Karnataka in the south of the Indian peninsula, is a good place to see elephants in the luxuriant forests and bamboo thickets which they most enjoy. Their total population in southern India is now about 12–13,000, nearly all living in the area where Karnataka, Tamil Nadu and Kerala adjoin in the shadow of the Western Ghats. Efforts are being made to prevent further encroachment on these wonderful forests.

Left: Very old elephants like this solitary old bull with a single tusk, are sometimes separated from the herd.

Bottom left: Shags and cormorants nest on skeletal trees in the drowned forest on the Kabbani River.

Bottom centre: *Panaeolus* – gill-bearing fungi growing on elephant droppings.

Bottom right: An elephant family makes its way through the forest in Nagarahole.

Below: A Brown Fish Owl showing its characteristic yellow eyes and streaked breast.

Above: A fully adult Gaur bull (shown with a pair of Mynahs on its back) would rarely be attacked by a Tiger, but calves are frequent victims.

Above left: The Nagarahole National Park provides an opportunity to see some of the southern population of Gaur or Indian Bison. The distinctive white feet and the high ridged shoulders of the bulls are shown clearly in this photograph.

Left: A species of parasitic *Cuscuta*, which slowly smothers its host.

Far left: A mating pair of Crimson Rose butterflies, *Pachiliopta hector*, which belong to the swallowtail group.

Centre left: Flowers of an *Aneilema* species.

Above: Three of India's colourful libellulid dragonflies: *Brachythemis contaminata* (top), *Neurothemis tullia* female (middle) and *Neurothemis tullia* male (bottom).

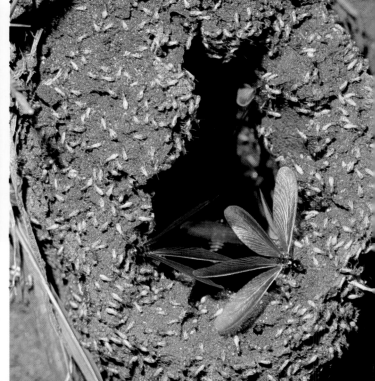

Top: A Sambar stag in the well-forested Bandipur National Park in Karnataka.

Above: Grey Junglefowl are widespread in southern India. This cock and hen were feeding at a termite nest, deftly catching the 'flying ants' as they emerged.

Right: A winged population of termites, *Odontotermes sp.*, emerge from their nest to create a new colony elsewhere.

Peafowl are common in the Bandipur National Park.
Like the Langur monkeys, they are constantly alert to
the approach of a Tiger or Leopard, and their
screaming alarm cries save many a deer or Wild Boar
from being caught. The peafowl on the right, with the
damaged train, may have been attacked by a Leopard.
These predators often try to catch peafowl at water-
holes and, if inexperienced, sometimes pounce on the
long train rather than the bird. When moulting, the
feathers of the train are dropped singly. The tail
beneath them is quite short.

Right: A group of Chital hinds in a grassy forest glade in the Mudumalai Sanctuary in Tamil Nadu.

Far right top: An adult male Chital calls to his hinds.

Far right centre: As the rutting season approaches, a Chital stag rubs its antlers against the back of a tree to cleanse them of remnants of 'velvet'.

Right: The tiny Mouse Deer, or Indian Chevrotain, is not much larger than a hare. Unlike true deer, this defenceless creature has four toes to each foot, and no antlers but, like the Musk Deer, it has short canine tusks. It occurs in the forested hills of southern, and some parts of central, India up to an elevation of about 1800 metres.

Centre right: A Spotted Owlet with a beetle it has just caught.

Bottom right: Well-camouflaged nestlings of the Red-wattled Lapwing.

Far right bottom: The flowers of a species of Curcuma.

Above: A colony of *Vespidae* social wasps on the surface of their paper nest.

Top: The forest is the habitat of the agile, long-limbed Langur monkeys.

Left: The rich, moist, deciduous forest of Mudumalai Sanctuary gives way in the south to the scrub vegetation of the Nilgiri Hills range.

Bonnet Macaque monkeys in the Mudumalai Sanctuary in Tamil Nadu. They are easily recognized by the untidy 'bonnets' of long hair radiating from their crowns. They are fairly numerous in southern India south of the Godavari River. Like the Rhesus Macaque in the north, they are usually very tame, and occupy most towns and villages, where they have an annoying and widespread habit of removing the tiles from roofs – perhaps in a search for insects. Many are trained by street beggars to perform tricks.

Right and below: There are many
distinctive varieties of the handsome
Indian Giant Squirrel. The variety found
in the moist evergreen forests of the
Malabar coastal region is black above and
bright reddish-orange below, whereas the
race in the dry deciduous forests at the
northern end of the Western Ghats is a
pale sandy colour. These large squirrels
(two and a half times larger than European
squirrels) spend most of their lives among
the higher branches, and are difficult to
observe closely. The squirrel on the right
is feeding on the flowers of a *Terminalia
crenulata* in the Mudumalai Sanctuary.

Above: By skilful management, the pools and streams in the Mudumalai Sanctuary have become perennial, to the great benefit of the wildlife. The trees are no longer lopped for firewood and beautiful scenes such as the one above are now common.

Centre left: An Indian Giant Squirrel.

Left: A male *Calotes* lizard displaying its inflated throat as a warning to rivals.

Left: The Moyar Gorge in the Nilgiri Hills is typical of the magnificent scenery of the southern region of the Indian peninsula.

Top: The delicate flowers of *Rhodomyrtus parviflora*.

Above: Many species of lizard, such as this yellow-necked Rock Lizard, *Psammophilus dorsalis*, inhabit the rocky gorges of the Nilgiri Hills.

Overleaf: The granitic crags of the Western Ghats rise dramatically from the edge of the plain.

Right: A nocturnal
Slender Loris.

Bottom left: Flowers
of *Cassia fistula* in the
forests of the Anamalai
Sanctuary.

Bottom right: Flowers of
an orange *Mussaenda sp.*

Left: A pair of Greater Flamebacks, a species of woodpecker. Note the chips flying as the upper bird 'drills' into the branch.

Below: A Sloth Bear beside its lair.

Right: A one-tusked Elephant bull emerges from Anamalai's Karian *shola* — temperate evergreen forest which is commonly associated with rolling grasslands above 1500 metres where it is found in patches.

Above: In the *shola* evergreen forest of the Anamalai Sanctuary, the rare Lion-tailed Macaques still maintain a stronghold. They can be found elsewhere only in the rain forests of the Ashambu Hills of the Western Ghats, and the Nellcampathi Hills in Kerala. Their shiny black fur, long, lion-like manes and tufted tails make them instantly recognizable. These monkeys are listed as an endangered species. In 1986 the toatal population was estimated to be 5,000, but it continues to decline with increasing fragmentation of the species' habitat.

Left: A forested landscape in the Anamalai Hills, which form part of the Western Ghats.

Above: The Kerala
Highlands near Munnar.

Right: The orchid
Dendrobium nanum.

Above: The Eravikulam National Park in the Kerala Highlands is the home of over 550 Nilgiri Tahr. These shy, sure-footed wild goats are restricted to the stony scarps at elevations of 1200 to 1850 metres. Slightly smaller than their Himalayan relatives, they have shorter, darker fur which in the older males is almost black, with a distinctive white saddle-patch across the loins.

Left: The purple flowering *Aristea ecklonii*, recorded for the first time in India, at an altitude of about 2000 metres in the Eravikulam National Park.

Above: Like all wild goats, Nilgiri Tahr have exceptionally keen eyesight, and can be approached only after arduous stalking across the barren slopes where they feed. During the heat of the day, they lie hidden among the rocks or higher levels, descending the slopes in the cool of dawn or evening. Their main enemy is the Leopard, which stalks them with great skill. Although their meat is not very palatable to humans, tahr were once hunted. Today, however, they are well protected in the highlands of Kerala and Tamil Nadu, the limit of their present distribution. The total population is estimated to be 2,000–2,500, but numbers are thought to be declining. All the other species of wild goats are restricted to northern India, and it is thought that the Nilgiri Tahr may have evolved from a population that was isolated by climatic changes which occurred many millions of years ago.

Top left: The buttress roots of a climbing fig.

Top right: Turtles bask on the bank of the Periyar River in the Periyar National Park.

Above: A colourful Dragonfly, *Trithemis aurora*.

Left: A predatory spider which has just caught a libellulid dragonfly, *Neurothemis tullia*, begins its meal by sucking the juices from the insect's head.

Far right: The Periyar Tiger Reserve is not large – only 777 square kilometres including its protective buffer zone – but it is important as it has plenty of water – especially from the dammed river. The Reserve is famous in southern India for its elephant herds, the activities of which can often be observed on the grassy shores of the huge lake. Sadly, relentless poaching has taken a heavy toll of the male tuskers', and today these are rarely seen. Periyar also embraces some of the finest tracts of undamaged wet-evergreen and semi-evergreen forest in southern India.

Top: Large numbers of deer, such as this Sambar herd, feed on the marshy borders of the lake in the Periyar Reserve, providing good prey for Tigers.

Above: Nilgiri Langurs are also numerous. Their black colouring, white ruffles and exceptionally long tails distinguish them from the Common Langur.

Overleaf: A palm-fringed shore at the southern tip of the Indian subcontinent.

INDEX